An Australian Country Childhood

ANDREW KENT

This book is dedicated to my parents and sisters who shared my childhood with me.

I am also extremely grateful to my daughter India without whose encouragement this book would not have been written, and also for her editing which has ensured that the audience is reading what was intended.

I would also like to thank and acknowledge Romney Nelson at Global Self-Publishing for ensuring it got published as intended.

Contents

Introduction

Every child thinks that their childhood is normal, and I was no exception. It is only many years later when time, parenthood and city life have given me a different perspective, that I recognised that my childhood was special.

This is not a story of sadness, hardship, success, redemption, or the backstory to someone famous. It is the story of a childhood rich in experiences as well as a time and way of living that has passed. It is as factual as my memory allows.

I enjoyed my childhood – I hope you enjoy it too.

Poorly Timed Arrival

I was born in Ballarat, Australia in August 1966, arriving a few weeks after decimal currency and a few weeks before St Kilda won its first VFL (now AFL) Premiership. More significantly for my parents, I arrived in the middle of shearing. Shearing was the busiest time of the year on their small sheep farm called Greenslopes, located in Haddon, 15 km west of Ballarat, and in the late 1960s moving shearing to another date was not an option.

The shearing team had been booked a year ahead and would not be available again for another year. The fact that we were shearing in the middle of winter was testament to the relatively low status of our farm. We were effectively stripping the sheep of their warm coats in the middle of winter – which was particularly harsh given Ballarat's reputation for being cold. It made getting them ready for shearing harder as well, because the wool needs to be dry before it is shorn, so if it was likely to rain we had to get them into the shed the night before so that they would be dry in the morning. The two shearers and the wool classer were particularly good at their jobs and prepared to work our small shed – which was a rare combination. Shearing is a hard life, physically demanding and involving constant travel between farms. Consequently, shearers are typically hard men. Part of the arrangement for hiring a shearing team was to provide them with morning and afternoon tea and a cooked sit-down lunch – as one of their few creature comforts, this was a high priority for them in choosing where they worked. This was also something usually provided by my mother, much to their satisfaction. However, due to my arrival, she was unavailable.

These responsibilities now fell on my maternal grandmother. Gran was a very capable woman, but certainly not used to the company of shearers. Although they owned a large farming property themselves, my maternal grandparents lived in the richest street in the richest suburb of Melbourne, and Gran was usually at least one person removed from the actual work. In her youth she had been a mid-wife, and she took it upon herself to stay with each of her six daughters when they were having a new-born. She would stay for several weeks and help the household in whatever way was needed. This did not usually extend to catering for the hired help – and during shearing it is not just the shearers who get fed. The farm also needs to provide a team to ensure that the shearer always has a sheep within grasp, and the wool from the sheep they have just shorn is cleared away and thrown across the wool classer's table. A shearer is paid by the number of sheep they shear, and so everything is done to make sure that they can shear as many as possible. At shearing time, only the wool classer is more important than a shearer. It is their job to class the wool into various grades to maximise the sale price of each wool bale – done well it can add a significant percentage to the value of the wool. As the income from the sale of the wool was most of the farm's annual revenue, this skill was highly valued. The wool classer at the time was very keen on a good spread at lunchtime – with a strong preference for large portions and second helpings. It was a preference that combined with a similar love of beer to produce a belly that almost prevented his arms from reaching the table.

It is difficult for anyone to cook well in an unfamiliar kitchen. In this case familiarity was just one of many difficulties. My parents had not inherited the farm, they had purchased it a couple of years earlier with a bank loan secured only with the backing of my maternal grandparents. In doing so they had chosen a farm that was affordable rather than good. The quality of a farm is usually measured on four things: its size, the quality of the soil, the reliability of the weather and the improvements (house, farm buildings, fences, dams, etc.). This farm was below par on all these measures. In real estate terms, it was a 'renovator's delight'. The kitchen itself was well past its prime.

The centrepiece of the kitchen was a rectangular table just large enough to seat six, one at each end and two either side. The room was also a rectangle of similar proportions to the table. When the chairs were pushed in under the table it was easy enough to walk around the room, but when people were seated it was a squeeze. The longer side of the room ran north south with the north end occupied by a chimney and the south end by the only door into the room. The eastern side of the kitchen had a bench and over-head cupboards. The western wall had a window that looked out over a small, gated vegetable garden, on the other side of which was a gravelled area onto which faced the shearing shed, sheep yards, machinery shed and wood heap.

Within the chimney was a coal-fired cast iron cooker that also heated the water for the house. It was kept running every moment of every day of the year. It had no controls for adjusting the temperature, that was done by adjusting the fuel and airflow to the fire and knowing which part of the stove top was the hottest. Level with the top of the cooker were some brick ledges on either side. These were used to rest the plates as the food was being dished out, and in lambing season often had a box in which new-born lambs struggling with the cold were placed to warm up. It was on this device Gran was required to prepare the prized cooked lunch.

The lunch story has been retold many times, each time with me being held responsible for my poorly timed arrival. So, I know that Gran was feeling pleased with her efforts prior to the arrival of these burly men into the tiny kitchen. Particularly given that my two older sisters, both under three years old at the time, had not made her task any easier. Nor did the fact that the wool classer chose to sit with his back to the chimney, apparently to warm his back. This put his chair closer to the cooker than the table, which put Gran dangerously close to the hot device as she dished the hot lunch onto their plates. This done, she placed the first plate in front of the wool classer, which is when the incident happened.

He picked up his knife and with one brisk stroke cleared his plate of peas, in the process firing the peas across the table, the room, and his fellow workers. At which point he simply stated, 'Don't like peas', and promptly started eating, blissfully unaware that Gran was standing behind him with a jug of hot gravy poised over his head. This prompted an exchange of meaningful looks between Gran and Dad, which when retold by the shearers who were present seemed to have taken an age and had them looking from Dad to Gran and back like a crowd on the side of a tennis match. As Gran retold it, the gravy was never destined for anything other than the table, but she had a mischievous streak, and I am not so sure. Dad certainly had his doubts. He was apparently thinking about how he could possibly get to the other end of the table in time to protect Gran from any harm if the wool classer responded poorly to having gravy on his head instead of his food – particularly given the proximity of the cooker.

As it transpired, the gravy was placed on the table and both lunch and the next few days of shearing continued without the wool classer ever being aware of how close he had come to having stove hot gravy poured over his head. Gran and Dad reached an understanding, peas were off the menu, and when shearing was over the wool classer was never coming back. The shearers and others present kept their silence that year. However, for many years after, if peas were served at lunch during shearing someone would set their knife ready to clear the plate of peas, prompting a chuckle and the retelling of the story so that even those who were not there, like me, could enjoy the retelling and the embellishments.

*****

I was the third born of four children in five years. My oldest sister Deborah (Debbie) was born in March 1963, Cynthia (Cindy) in December 1964, and my younger sister Barbara (Barb) in February

1968, which was a drought year on the farm. I was too young to remember much of that drought, but I do remember bath time.

Even in good times, water is a valuable commodity on a farm, particularly in Australia. Rainwater is collected off roofs and stored in water tanks wherever possible. The tanks are interconnected so that they can all feed drinkable water into the house and other places it is needed. In 1968, the tanks were low, and were being supplemented by water pumped from one of our dams that was also being used by the farm animals and getting low itself.

Farm kids get dirty, and the only way to stop everything in the house from getting dirty as well, particularly the beds, was a daily bath. It was a shared experience, the kids, then Mum, then Dad, with top ups of hot water from the kettle on the stove in between. The water was shallow and not particularly clean to begin with, add kids, dirt and lots of soap and the water was opaque. Like many families of the era we have photos of kids in the bath, my sisters and I and various combinations of cousins all grinning happily because bath time was fun time.

It was on one of these occasions during that drought year, when just after Mum had finished bathing my baby sister Barb, that my older sisters and I took over the bath while it was still relatively warm. The problem was that we could not find the soap. This was not unusual, and as the one closest to the free-standing wash basin that was next to the bath, it fell to me to stand up and look in the basin for the soap. Given the water was warm and the air was cold, this was a task to be done as quickly as possible. I found the bar of soap instantly - by standing on it in the bath. It was a surprise discovery that threw me off balance, causing my chin to crash down on the edge of the basin on my way back into the bath, which proceeded to turn red with my blood. My sisters and I screamed, and my Mum rushed back into the bathroom to so much noise and blood covered children that she was not sure what had happened. Eventually she calmed the situation but could not stem the bleeding, I was taken to the hospital in Ballarat to have the wound treated and sewn up. I still have a scar with the stitch-marks under my chin.

It is one of the ironies of those early years that of all the dangerous and risky things we did, it was a block of soap in the bath that caused the hospital visit. My parent's general approach to safety was that we (the kids) were to stay together and if anything went wrong then one of us was to go and get help. Given that we were on an Australian farm with poisonous spiders and snakes as well as feral cats, electric fences, unfenced dams and the many other potential hazards of farm life, this approach might appear reckless to the modern parent. But it worked remarkably well, and a generation later I saw my cousin adopt the same approach with her kids on her farm and it worked just as well for them.

One of the benefits of this approach is that giving kids responsibility makes them responsible. It also taught us how to work together, to find solutions and balance risk and reward. We did not always get it right, but we certainly grew up with an underlying confidence that we would find a way to deal with whatever came along. But learning must start somewhere, and one of my early lessons as a pre-school kid is that life is different to cartoons.

What led me to this conclusion started out as a visit from one of Mum's old school friends and her only child. He was about my age, and so we were expected to get along. It must have been a year or so after the bath incident as both my older sisters were at school, and Barb was old enough to walk and talk. After spending some time inside the house near our mothers we left them to go outside and ride the tricycles. We had two tricycles, one of them was larger and had a seat at the back for a passenger. When playing with my sisters, one kid would ride the solo tricycle, while the other three would team up on the two-seater tricycle – my little sister Barb in the back, someone pedalling and someone pushing. We did laps of the house in this manner and had a lot of fun doing it.

The house was situated within a small, fenced garden. The house had a front and back door, although the front door was rarely used and neither door was ever locked. The kitchen was at the back of the house as was the laundry and a small, covered veranda that also functioned as what Americans call a mudroom – full of boots and coats and things that are too dirty to go inside. It was practical but ugly and it was the entrance to the house used 99% of the time. It had been commented on disparagingly by my mother's guest earlier in the day, but more on that later. Outside of this were several paths, one leading to the clothesline, another to the back gate (really the main gate, as it led to everything including the woolshed), and some smaller paths that led to either side of the house and various parts of the vegetable garden. At the side of the house the paths also connected to the front veranda which was elevated and wrapped around the 'front' of the house. At this end of the house there was a picket fence around the garden, and between this fence and the veranda, rose bushes that had not been attended to for many years.

Our preferred tricycle track incorporated the side paths and the veranda to create a lap of the house. Barb and I suggested to our guest that we all use the two-seater tricycle so that we could all be part of it – I even volunteered to do the pushing. However, our guest had other ideas and chose to ride the single seater tricycle on his own. This left Barb and I as spectators as I was not big enough to ride the two-seater tricycle on my own. However, he was the guest, and we were raised to give the guest first preference, and, in this case, this meant first turn. Once again, our guest had other ideas, thirty minutes in it was apparent that he had no intention of giving us a turn. Barb and I were unhappy about this and knowing that Mum would just repeat that we should look after our guest, decided to take matters into our own hands. This kid had to be stopped.

Inspired by Coyote from the *Roadrunner* cartoon I decided that glue was the answer. Entering the house through the rarely used front door I went into the office and grabbed a large bottle of Clag – a type of paper glue. One of the things about farm life is that everything is purchased in bulk, and the Clag was no exception – I had trouble carrying the bottle. I waited inside the front door until our guest went past, then I rushed out onto the veranda to set my trap for his next lap. I clumsily poured the contents of the full bottle of Clag over the veranda so that when he came around the corner the next time, he would get stuck and I would finally have my turn.

So, I was as surprised as anyone that instead of the glue stopping the tricycle it caused him to slide. Indeed, he slid quite dramatically off the veranda and landed upside down in the rose bushes with the tricycle on top of him. He screamed, cried, and carried on and so our mothers promptly arrived. Once they had extracted him from the roses it was not hard for them to determine what happened. The large patch of glue with wheel tracks through it combined with my guilty face would have been evidence enough, but what closed out the case was that Barb gave an accurate account of events. I was sent to my room to be dealt with later, while our guests decided it was time to leave.

As it turned out I got off without punishment, which was a rare thing. Standard punishment in our house was being hit on the backside with the wooden spoon or hairbrush. The worse the crime the higher the number of hits, the other variation was how hard – younger meant softer. If we got in trouble together, we would have to line up to be punished. On another occasion we had all lined up only for Mum to break the hairbrush on Cindy who was first in line, so the rest of us got off – which Cindy rightly said was unfair. I found out later that the reason I was not punished for the tricycle incident was that Mum was as unhappy with her guest as Barb and I were with ours.

As I mentioned, Mum grew up in wealthy circles. Which meant that most of her acquaintances were from rich families. It is my opinion that wealth is the ultimate test of character, and it is a test that most people fail. Mum was one of six sisters, all of them were fashionably attractive for the period, and with money and connections were expected to marry well. Mum was the fourth oldest and looked remarkably similar to the third oldest, named Margaret. The differences were subtle but significant. Margaret was stunning and charming while Mum was the quiet but attractive girl next door. As young children Dad had courted Margaret. It was only holding hands, but it still cast a shadow. By the standards of their circles Dad was reasonable, but not a great catch. He was respectable in that he was from a respectable family – his grandfather was the longest serving chairman of the Melbourne Stock Exchange and a founder of Trinity College. Dad had also been in the Scotch College first crew in rowing for two years and was an engineering student when they got engaged. But he had left engineering to follow his newfound passion for farming that led to him managing my mother's parents' property "Wooloomanata" before they purchased their own farm. My mother and her guest had spent time together at Wooloomanata as children. This was a property ten times the size of my parents' farm which also featured a grand bluestone homestead that was big enough to have been used by the Airforce as accommodation and offices during the Second World War. I am not entirely sure what Mum's guest was expecting but she had clearly let my mother know that our house was well below an acceptable level to her, and that it was further evidence that

Mum had chosen poorly in marriage. It was the last contact Mum had with her and I think she was pleased that I had provided a reason to bring an abrupt end to the acquaintance.

It certainly did not put an end to my mischief. Not long after this, Mum decided that I had done something that did deserve the wooden spoon. I don't recall why I was in trouble, but my older sister Debbie recalls that she and Cindy were on the swings near the back of the house when the back door crashed open and I came sprinting out with fists and legs pumping, followed closely by Mum with wooden spoon in hand. The chase proceeded around various objects in the garden until Mum stopped out of breath and started laughing, at which point I raised my arms in triumph with a cheeky grin on my face.

Cheeky was the most frequent description of me as a child. I always took it as a compliment, although I am sure it was not always intended as one. It certainly helped me to get away with things. The local primary school was about 50 metres north of our house, with our horse paddock in between. As kids we were free to roam near the house, including in the horse paddock. We had three horses at the time – a shetland pony and two stock horses. They were good natured and accustomed to our presence and were often fed apples and bread by the school kids from their lunchboxes. With my two older sisters at school, I sometimes made my way across the horse paddock to see them at recess and lunch time. On one of these occasions, I ran straight under the belly of one of the larger horses in my rush to see them. This entertained the other school kids, so with their encouragement I did it again. It would become my party trick for visiting cousins and guests for a few years – the whole time I was blissfully unaware that each run through was greeted with a kick from the horse. Which goes to show what a fine line there is between bravery and ignorance – they thought I was brave; I was simply ignorant of the danger. I was also unaware that my pre-school days were going to be cut short.

Haddon Primary School

Haddon was a place in name only. It had a primary school and a post office one kilometre apart and nothing of any distinction between or around them other than a railway siding of the same name. Prior to the First World War it had a larger population based on the gold mining activity in the area. Testament to this was that there were more soldiers from the district who died in the First World War listed on the honour boards in the primary school than people who now lived in the district.

The school building in which the honour boards were displayed had been built in the 1800s as a two-room school. Accompanying it in one corner of the two-acre grounds was the schoolteacher's house, of the same vintage as the buildings, which was made available to the school principal and his family as one of the perks of the job. This also made them our closest neighbour by some distance.

But it was our next-door neighbour on the other side of the property who would play a significant role in the future of the school. This property was unsettled land owned by two prominent Ballarat families who operated the preeminent legal firm in Ballarat for many years. One of them, Murray, was also a member of the Victorian Parliament and as luck would have it for Haddon, the Minister for Public Works in the late 1960s. Now the following story might vary from the truth a little as when among friends Murray was not one to let the truth stand in the way of a good story, and this version of events is based on his telling of it, as I was too young to have any part of it.

Murray and Dad had met over the fence between our properties and from that conversation a life-long friendship developed. Murray was good at talking and Dad was good at listening and both preferred not to take themselves or life too seriously. It was through this friendship that the Haddon community managed to get the attention of the education minister regarding the plight of the local school. The community wanted a new classroom for the school, declaring that the old building was designed for a previous century and was inappropriate for the modern age. According to Murray, this was not enough to convince the Education Department, so after some discussion and debate with the local community the old building was declared uninhabitable to justify the need for the new classroom to be built. Then Murray was given a new challenge, to save the old building from being demolished.

The logic of the education department was straight forward; if the building is uninhabitable it should be removed from the school grounds as it would be a hazard to the students. So, the community had to pull together to do just enough work on the building to make to usable, but not enough to remove the need for the new (and only) classroom. With the support of the education minister, this fine line was navigated, and the school retained a building in which they could gather for various social events and school plays, and in which the kids could play indoors in winter. After retelling the story Murray would argue with much laughter that it was one of his greatest political achievements to declare a building uninhabitable and irreparable and then turn around and save it as a community treasure within the same year.

His accomplishment was nearly short lived. As the 1971 school year loomed, the school did not have enough students to remain open. Once again, the community rallied, and this time I was central to the solution – I was to be enrolled in the school early. The justification for this was that I had been a sickly child who was surely going to miss many school days during my school years and subsequently be kept down a year at some point, which would result in me finishing school in the correct year. It was a story told to me in case anybody asked, and despite the fact that I had been a firsthand witness to my own health and wellbeing, it was a story I believed so completely that even years later I thought it was true.

The year I joined the school there were 15 other kids from six families spread across prep to grade six. We were all taught by a single teacher in the school's only classroom with occasional assistance from local mothers. Having looked at the school over the fence I was not worried about joining my sisters, even if I was the only Prep kid. Fortunately, I was reasonably bright for my age and the classwork was not a problem – other than perhaps my spelling and handwriting, which are two skills that have been below par my entire life. Time outside the classroom was more challenging.

School in the '70s was physical, particularly in the country. We were all farm kids accustomed to physical activity and many of my fellow students did not enjoy the classroom. To combat this the teacher had us start each day by running a lap of the school, sometimes two. Also, the class reward for good behaviour in the morning was sport in the afternoon. At recess and lunch none of the school was out of bounds. We climbed trees, played hide-and-seek by hiding in long grass (checking first for snakes), squeezed between gaps in buildings and fences (checking first for spiders) and generally ran amok. I think the teacher hoped that we would wear ourselves out, but we simply got fitter. Possibly because of this the school often won the district school sports, which also had a points adjustment based on the number of children in each school.

It was at the district sports in my first year of school that I remember my first official race. All the races were arranged by distance and age, starting with the older kids and working down. Each school had a lane and we lined up waiting for our turn to run. There was lots of organising being done by adults who were strangers to me, and I recall getting more and more nervous as each race passed. Because we were a small school, there were also races in which we had no runners. As the youngest in the school there were several races between my sister's race (Cindy was the next youngest in the school) and mine. I sat waiting patiently but nervously, as more and more kids sprinted down the track away from me. Then just after one of the races had departed, I looked around to realise I was the only one left. I must have missed the start of my race!

I jumped up and sprinted after them, tears streaming down my face as I tried to catch up. I did not want to be the one to let the school down. I need not have worried. I was the only kid in my age group. I arrived to be smothered in sympathy from various mothers who thought that it was all very cute. I also received a ribbon for coming first and a barley sugar for coming last. And later that day the school was once again awarded the district sports trophy.

One of the reasons the school kept winning was a family of great runners who would be at the school for 23 consecutive years. They had nine children – four boys, then a girl, then four boys. The girl, Liz, was in the year above me along with Cindy and the two of them were my school friends. Although to them I was probably the third wheel. It was this friendship that got me into my first fight. A grade three boy, Peter was keen on Liz and not happy about the amount of time I spent with her. I don't remember much about the fight, it was very one sided, but I have a vivid image of him sitting on my chest and punching me about the face – and the thing that I remember most about it was that he was crying. I remember being puzzled about it because I could not remember hitting him at all. Fighting was not uncommon between the boys at the school and usually it was the person losing, as I certainly was, that did the crying.

Being the smallest in the school also meant that you were put in places by the bigger kid to climb out on the end of tree limbs to fetch stuck balls, and inside various containers just to see if you could fit. At one point in time, the game at the school was rolling an old, corrugated iron water tank down the hill with the smaller kids inside and the bigger kids pushing. The water tank had no top and a rusted through bottom that scythed around as the tank rolled down the hill on its side. The challenge for those of us inside was to try and run as fast the tank, because once you lost your footing it was a violent ride for the rest of the way. Usually someone lost their footing and toppled everyone else. The bigger kids seemed to think that this was very amusing and would try and get the tank rolling as fast as possible to make this happen. Eventually someone got hurt badly enough for the adults to care and the old water tank was taken away.

The two school excursions I remember also provide an insight into the limited resources of the school. The first was a short walk to our farm to watch one of the horses give birth to a foal. The second was to spend a day at a larger primary school in Ballarat. This school not only had more than one classroom, it also had more than one classroom per year level and hundreds of kids. I think the idea behind it was to help prepare the older kids for high school. After being paraded in front of the school at assembly as a kind of welcome and explanation to the other kids as to why we were there, we were sent to the relevant classroom for our year level. For me as the only Prep it was terrifying. Things did not improve in the classroom as the teacher had some troublesome kids to attend to and all the other kids were too focused on their own lives to give me any assistance. Recess was spent unsuccessfully trying to find my sister, and lunchtime was spent trying to find the toilet. I finished the day certain that I never wanted to attend a big school.

I only spent two years attending Haddon Primary School, and so the rest of my memories of it relate more to it as our neighbour. The reason being that by the end of my grade one year some more young families had moved into the district, so Mum decided to send us to a larger school in Ballarat – more on that later.

It seems that small country schools attract characterful teachers. Shortly after I left, a new teacher arrived with his wife, a young son and two dogs: a Great Dane and a Bloodhound. On a still night in the country, you can hear for miles around, which means dogs from neighbouring farms easily get set off and start barking at each other. The Bloodhound was not discriminating, and he was loud. He rarely barked, but he howled long sorrowful howls frequently enough that our sheep dogs got used to it and began to ignore him.

The teacher before him had also been famous for their dog. I don't recall it, possibly because we never drove to the school, but people in the district loathed it. The reason for this was that, unlike most country dogs that greet visiting cars by running around them barking, this little dog waited for the cars to stop before going under the car. Once a person put one foot out of the car, the dog would bite them around the ankle – usually while the other leg was still inside the car. On one such occasion two local farmers arrived in the same vehicle and stepped out either side at the same time. The dog bit one of them, then rushed across to bite the other. The second farmer went to swing his foot out of the way of the unseen assassin but instead scooped the dog up with such a well-timed stroke that the dog landed on the roof of the teacher's house, startled but unhurt. Even though it was an accident, he was praised and thanked for it by the district as it stopped the dog from biting people ever again.

The next teacher and his wife also had a dog, a beagle cross which was usually fat from overeating. When they arrived, they were a young couple with no kids. The reason I remember they had a dog is because we were required to look after it while they were away on a camping holiday. This was no big deal, until the dog decided to go under their house to give birth to her puppies and sounded very much like she was in trouble. Because we were just feeding the dog and collecting their mail, we did not have keys to the house. We resolved this in the usual manner – by getting Dad. After a number of failed attempts to get the dog to come to us, he decided we would need to go to the dog. To achieve this, he levered open the backdoor, breaking the lock in the process. Once inside, we estimated what part of the house the dog was under, then moved the furniture out of the way, and ripped up the floorboards. We then extracted the dog and her puppies and took them back to our house. So you can imagine their surprise when they returned home to find the door broken in and further inside a major hole in the middle of their wooden floor. In addition to this, they could not find the dog, because we had her and her puppies safely up at our house. They were the last people to live at the school. He stayed on as school principal for over 20 years, but they purchased a house outside the school catchment and raised their family there outside the gaze of the school parents and students. Privacy can be hard to find in the country, particularly on still nights.

Family

A family farm is a family business and so country families are both siblings and work colleagues, and this starts from a young age. I don't remember learning to ride a horse, probably because I was in the saddle when I was less than two years old. I know this because there is a photo of me on the back of our Shetland pony which was being led by Mum. So, learning to ride was not an event, but a transition in which you were judged to be good enough to go to the next level, eventually being good enough to ride the stock horses while herding the bulls.

Most of life on the farm was like that, a gentle progression of role and responsibility founded on experience and capability. People are accustomed to seeing tradesmen with dogs that they take from job to job with the dog sitting and watching them while they work. In the country as a young child, I had a similar role to the dog. I was taken everywhere and watched and waited while things went on around me. I watched the shearing for years before I had an active role. By the time I was given a role I already knew what was expected of me.

One time as a pre-school kid I accompanied Dad and a neighbouring farmer while they built a fence. It was summer, and the metal trailer got too hot to sit on, so it was decided to put me on the ground in the shade on a bare patch where there were no snakes or spiders. They continued constructing the fence a little way away until my screaming and yelling got their attention. They had left me on a bull-ants nest and by the time they returned I was covered in bull ants (which have a very nasty sting) and welts. Being at least 15 minutes from the house, they decided the best solution was to put me in the nearest dam. I was horrified, I could not swim and felt that things were just getting worse and worse. I cried and resisted, but they prevailed. Fortunately, it worked. The ants did not like being submerged and the cool water eased the pain of the stings. As for my fear of drowning, I need not have worried, Dad held me the entire time.

Within the house Mum had a more proactive approach to learning, which she called 'training for independence'. She was passionate about this process because she did not want us to have the same experience as her, as she had left home not knowing how to do any of the household chores, because they had all been done for her. She had Dad's full support in this as he recalled his own mother having the same issues in relation to her transition from home. What possibly set us apart from other households was how young we started.

I remember being in the little kitchen with wooden kitchen chairs lined up against the sink and bench, the seats providing a scaffolding platform, and the back of the seats a safety rail. Standing on the chairs enabled us to reach the sink, so that we could wash and dry the dishes. One washed, two dried, one put away (usually from ground level) – there was a roster, and we all took turns. While we often complained about having to do the dishes, we generally had fun doing it. The task itself would become background, almost autopilot while we chatted and laughed. It was often the last thing we did before the younger ones were sent to bed. Bedtimes were set by age, with Barb and I going to bed earlier than the other two, even though we all slept in the same room.

It was during one of our dish-doing sessions that we hatched a plot to trick the babysitter. Mum and Dad were in their room getting ready to go out, and the babysitter was yet to arrive, so we were able to talk freely. The babysitter was a nice teenage girl from one of the neighbouring farms, a very trustworthy but distinctly indoor girl. We all liked her, so the trick was designed for entertainment not malice. A central part of the plot was that Barb and I had already gone to bed. I don't recall where Barb was, but my part of the trick was to hide in the cupboard under the kitchen sink and make scratching noises like a rat. Deb and Cindy would draw attention to the scratching and suggest that the babysitter needed to do something about it. We had not thought much beyond that when we put the plan into action.

Everything went to plan; but the plan lacked a conclusion. It certainly did not include the babysitter arming herself with the fire poker. Fortunately, my sisters provided a running commentary of what the babysitter was doing. So, as I heard my sisters commentating on which of the two doors under sink cupboards the babysitter was about to open, I would scuttle to the other side to remain undetected, which gives some indication as to how small I must have been. Tension built inside and outside the cupboard. My sisters talked up the size of the rat, while inside the cupboard I was worried about the poker and struggling to keep up with which side of the cupboard I was meant to be on. Eventually, both doors were opened at the same time, and I leapt out yelling. This startled the babysitter who jumped back and dropped the fire poker. After the adrenaline had subsided, we all had a good laugh together before Barb and I went off to bed.

Our bedroom was under a skillion roof to the south side of the house, it was an addition built by my parents and included two second-hand floor-to-ceiling sash windows. At either end of the room were two bunk beds which we slept in. Next to these were the sash windows, and in between the sash windows was a single bed. When our cousins came to stay, two foldout beds were added to this arrangement, one placed in front of each of the windows, so that the room could sleep seven.

This is one of the things about country visitors, they usually stay a while. If it is going to take you a day to get there and a day to get home again, you want to make the trip worthwhile. My dad was the youngest of four siblings, my mother the fourth of six siblings. We had 24 cousins, and because they came and went as families, we related to them more as a mini collective than individuals. We saw some of the cousins more than others, with those closest to us geographically and by age seen more often than those significantly older, younger, or further away. On one visit from our most frequent visitors, David and Sarah, the guest comes first rule caused some tension in relation to bed choices.

When guests came to stay, which kid slept in which bed was shuffled and reallocated by some system that I never understood. On this occasion I got one of the top bunks, which I thought was a treat. Meanwhile my two older sisters and my two older cousins were allocated the lower beds and the foldout beds – I am not exactly sure who got what, but I do know that Sarah got one of the folding beds and my sister Debbie wanted it. Debbie knew not to dispute the guest comes first rule, so she took matters into her own hands and set a mouse trap within the sheets when she made up the folding beds prior to our cousins' arrival.

Much later, and after much excitement, it was time for bed. At which point Sarah, a very down to earth character, found out that Debbie was disappointed not to have been allocated one of the folding beds. With a minimum of fuss, she offered to swap beds, which pleased Debbie no end. So, Debbie got into the folding bed and sprung her own trap by putting her foot into the mouse trap. Her screams brought my parents into the room to demand who had put the mouse trap into the bed – with a lot of suspicion directed my way. In between sobs, Debbie admitted that it was her.

Our farm was a popular place among our cousins and as we grew older, our friends. I put a lot of its appeal down to my father – Bob. A farm is like most businesses in that its culture reflects the personality of the CEO, in this case, my dad. To give you an understanding of the man, I will share with you the eulogy I wrote for his funeral.

Farmer Bob Tribute, 2010

I would like to share with you all a sense of my father, Bob, during the farm years.

From a young father in his mid-twenties through to his 50th birthday dad was a farmer, they were important years. You have already heard of his many achievements during this time, but always with Dad, the outcome was only a small part of the story.

Dad always took his responsibilities seriously and ensured the job was done well, but I always got the sense with him that having fun was just as important. For Dad, fun meant people, and the more the merrier. Growing up mum and dad always encouraged us to have friends stay at the farm during the school holidays, which also coincided with key farm activities, particularly cattle work. My sisters and I were his main work force during these busy periods, assisted by our friends or in some cases entertained by our friend's efforts to assist. It was a farm and a house full of noise and activity and at the eye of the storm was Dad – forever calm and smiling.

Many of our friends and cousins got their first taste of farming with us. Like us they were always encouraged to try new things, many rode their first horse, drove their first car, tractor, and threw their first hay bale with us. Each of these milestones were a source of joy not only to the individual, but also for Dad. He had an unswerving and infectious belief in people. His belief made people feel stronger and challenges smaller. Nothing seemed impossible in dad's presence.

He was always quick to laugh. It is possibly the only thing he did quickly. He lived in the moment. If you were with him it was wonderful, the world was a joyful place. If you were waiting for him in an era before mobile phones it taught you patience. It was not unusual for him to be late picking us up from school, but he set a record at the end of one winter's term when we were dismissed at noon and sat waiting at the school gates for him, but did not see him until 6pm that night. It is a story we told in his presence many times, and he would always laugh. With Dad it did not matter if he was the source of the joke, so long as there was laughter and joy to be shared. It was impossible to stay mad with him, even as a teenager.

Dad was innovative and open to new ideas. As you have heard he was a trail-blazer in beef farming. In doing so he had to put academic theory into practice. It is one thing to have the birth weight of a calf in a formula, but another thing to be chased by a cow while trying to hold its newborn calf in the air. One thing to select bulls based on their past performance, another to pregnancy test each cow at the right time to know which bull actually did the performance. He was prepared to do the hard yards when many around him were not.

Innovations were a constant source of joy for dad. He was very proud of his numerous inventions and gadgets. One of his favourite inventions was a bespoke fire-grate constructed from exhaust pipes which curved around to pump heat back into the room. It worked well – until a few years later when a hole burnt through one of the pipes and suddenly pumped lots of smoke into the living room.

Another was a mobile viewing platform for the eight kids he took from Ballarat to Melbourne to watch his beloved Hawks. It gave us all a great view, although it did require us to carry in a 6 foot timber plank through the turnstiles and past the crowds. We got some heckling from the other football goers, but true to his nature Dad would respond by laughing with them.

As a father, he encouraged each of us to follow our dreams and pursue our passions. He asked only that we have a go and do our best. He wanted us to experience a wide variety of things. At least that was his excuse for frequently taking me out of school to travel with him to field days, shows, wool sales and cattle studs. Perhaps he was right - I can still remember some of these trips, although I am not sure of the educational value of knowing that in addition to breakfast, lunch, dinner, drinks and snacks, at a field day in Hamilton, a father and son can also eat 12 choc wedge ice creams each.

On a serious note - being around Dad was educational. In his company I learnt about leadership; humanity; humility; nature; and anything else I wanted to ask about. His lessons were life lessons. He showed me what a father could be. He showed me that the joy of life was everywhere, all the time. He lived life brightly, brilliantly. We miss him dearly.

The thought of Dad dying never crossed my mind in those early years. He was so full of life it seemed impossible that he would ever run out of it. Unfortunately for Mum, who was older and wiser than I, the possibility of him dying was much closer than she would have liked. He gave her several close scares that as a young mother she would have preferred to do without.

As I mentioned earlier, our farm was not a good one. So, like many of our neighbouring farmers, my parents needed to have another job. Mum was a qualified physiotherapist and worked part time at one of the Ballarat hospitals. In most of these early years, Dad's other job was managing my grandparents' farm – which was two hours drive away. However, for a short period of time he took a job helping to construct the offshore oil rigs in Bass Straight. He was officially employed as a rigger, but unofficially he was helping one of his school friends, whose family engineering business was helping with construction. They were having people problems out on the rigs that they could not get to the bottom of, so Dad's main objective was to find out why. But Dad never did anything half-heartedly, so committed to his cover story, he set up scaffolding without any safety gear, suspended above a surging ocean on a swaying oil rig. Fortunately, he returned home unscathed. However, the stories others told of Dad jumping up and down to test his scaffolding ahead of it being used by the riggers gave Mum nightmares for years. He did find out the reason for the people issues as well – high stakes gambling. Men were betting and losing their houses at poker during recreation hours on the rigs.

It was an accident on our farm, which occurred before I was born, that left Dad unable to run. He was riding a horse around dusk when it was spooked by something, reared up and threw Dad from its back. Unfortunately, one of his feet got stuck in the stirrup, which caused his ankle joint to be pulled apart as the horse bolted. He was nearly a kilometre from home and riding alone at the time, so it was a slow and painful walk back. Dad's ankle was later fused together in surgery. It enabled him to walk normally, but anything beyond that was awkward and painful. It also meant that for the rest of his life he slept with a pillow at the bottom of the bed to keep the weight of the bedding off his ankle. It certainly did not stop him getting back on the horse, although a few years later he found a type of stirrup with a safety release to prevent a foot being caught in the same way. He was quick to have these fitted to all the saddles on the farm.

Dad was also involved in a bad car accident on one of his trips to my grandparents' property, Wooloomanata, as part of his manager's role there. A permanent reminder of this was a slightly bent nose. But I think it gave Mum more scars than Dad. In addition to his disregard for his own safety, he was also notorious for having a disregard for time, and Mum was prone to worry. It was a combination that gave her many anxious hours.

On each of the occasions when Dad was out of action, Mum was required to step into the breach and keep things moving forward. It was something she always did well. So much so that I think she appears calmer and more comfortable in a crisis than when things are going well. Perhaps she finds it easier to deal with the crisis in front of her than the many potential crises in her mind.

Mum is the only woman I know who enjoyed pregnancy. She said that this is the reason she had four kids in five years. I don't think she enjoyed looking after four young children as much. There were at least two occasions on which we pushed her past her limit and she very dramatically ran away from home. I say dramatically, because she put on a show, telling us that we needed to behave better, that she could not cope, making sure we all saw her packing a suitcase. The suitcase seemed to require items from different rooms in the house so that the whole production took a good deal of time. She even drove away, leaving us alone in the house waiting for Dad to return from the farm, (apparently, she just drove around to the front of the school where we could not see her – but we did not know that). After she left, we would do our best to make the house tidy and erase any obvious misdemeanours. By the time Dad got home, we would be sitting quietly as though it was impossible to think that we could have done anything to cause Mum any distress.

The first time this happened I was concerned about how Dad was going to react. So, when he calmly set about making us dinner and getting us off to bed. I was very confused as to why he was not more stressed, (apparently he had already seen Mum on his way home, so he was not the least bit concerned). The second time it happened, we were also more relaxed, so much so that I am not sure she attempted it a third time.

Dad's injuries and young children were not the only source of stress for my parents. A few years after the drought, the farm's sheep flock got footrot – an infectious condition that causes the hoof to split and tear and prevents the sheep from walking. Because it is infectious, it also prevents the farmer from selling the sheep in the stock yards. As it would quickly spread to other farms via other sheep that had been through the same yards, it is illegal to take sheep with the condition to market. Unfortunately, somebody did, which is how our farm ended up with it. During a drought, farmers reduce their stock numbers, then once the drought is over, they top up by buying new stock. The new stock we acquired did not have footrot, but they picked up the disease from the sale yards and introduced it to our farm, and once on a farm it can take years to get rid of it.

My parents did what they could to try and keep the flock intact. Part of this involved running the sheep through troughs of chemical treatment. This was done in the yards behind the shearing shed, but as kids we were not allowed anywhere near it – the chemicals were harsh. One of our neighbours had some splash onto his tongue and was permanently scarred from it. Another part of the treatment was rotating the sheep through paddocks in a controlled fashion, with a foot bath in between and not returning to the old paddock for several months. Ideally the paddocks are used by other livestock, not sheep, in between. My parents purchased some cows for this purpose. This was the inconspicuous start to my parents becoming beef farmers.

A few years later the only sheep we had were those Dad had kept for us to eat. They were all young at the time they were chosen, the best yearling lambs. Dad kept over twenty of them, but we only ate about four a year, and over time they get older, bigger, and not so good to eat. There is a saying about mutton dressed up as lamb, well the last of these were mutton no matter how well they were dressed.

The two who were saddest about the sheep going were the sheep dogs. James and Shep, both had been trained by Dad before I was born and were amazing to watch working the sheep. Dad would send them this way and that like two remote control cars using a series of whistles. The dogs loved it; you will not see a happier dog than a good sheep dog at work.

Change in Fortune

While there were no sheep on our farm, there were still plenty on my grandparents' farm Wooloomanata - several thousand of them. As Dad was the farm manager, the dogs sometimes joined him on his trips there, although as the farm also had a team of farm hands and dogs this was not a requirement. That could also be said of us as kids – at home we were part of the workforce, at Wooloomanata we were extras – which meant that we did things we would not have done at home, particularly if our cousins were also there.

One of these things was Ram Rodeo – a creation of my cousin David. A scaled down version of a real rodeo for adults and bulls, it was a competition to see who could stay on the back of the ram the longest – providing the ram was moving. The rams were Merinos, and they were about to be shorn – so they were a sizable bundle of wool and muscle happy to use their signature curled horns to keep us away. I was the smallest, which meant that it was harder for me to catch and mount the ram, but it also meant that the ram kept moving. David was the biggest and so his problem was finding a ram that did not simply stop as soon as he mounted it.

The shearing shed itself was one of the largest in the state, classified by the National Trust – it was immense when not in use, and a hive of activity during shearing. With over a dozen shearers and multiple wool classing tables, it was an entirely professional operation. I recall being perched on wool bales watching the action, in awe of the ceaseless movement and unspoken integration and synchronisation of all the moving parts.

Where our farm, Greenslopes, was small and under resourced with poor farming land, Wooloomanata was the opposite. Everything about it was on a grand scale, and the remnants of its use by the Airforce during the Second World War were exciting to us as kids. One of these was the phone system in the homestead.

The homestead had been converted into a combination of officers quarters and headquarters of some sort during the war, and while I cannot tell you what they used the various rooms for, I can tell you that they left behind a phone system with multiple phone lines all in different rooms and able to dial each other. The building was bluestone and single-story in a U shape, with the bottom of the U being longer and facing south, and the inside of the U facing onto a large quadrangle. This structure had an old and very grand stable on the north side. It would have been the rear of the homestead, but because that was where the cars were parked, it was also where we entered from – generally through the kitchen which was on the eastern side of the quadrangle. Along the southern side was a raised veranda with iron lattice work and bluestone steps at its midpoint that lead down to what may have been a garden at some time but was just a paddock as I recall it.

Within the house a long hall ran east to west and was close to 100 metres long. At its mid-point it branched north and south to a sunroom on one side and the veranda on the other. At the western end it turned north and provided access to a grand ballroom about the size of a basketball court. In between these feature rooms were lots of doors that opened on to mostly bedrooms, but also some bathrooms and a plant room and some rooms we were not allowed into. It was in this setting that my cousin Sarah invented phone tag. One person would dial a phone, and the rest would run through the homestead trying to get to it before it stopped. If you were the first one there, then it was your turn to ring another phone. There were only three numbers we were not allowed to dial – the office, the kitchen, and the lounge room – all occupied by adults. The tricky part was that what labels did exist on the phone had been put there by the air force, and meant nothing to us, so we had to memorise which rooms they belonged to. We had a lot of fun playing various versions of the game as well as hide and seek and all the other games that small kids like to play in large houses with lots of friends.

Because Dad was farm manager, we spent more time at Wooloomanata than the other cousins, but it was always more fun for us when they were there. There were also times when he was called there unexpectedly. One of these was when the lagoon dam wall burst during a heavy rain, which caused flash flooding as it travelled downstream, even swelling the banks of the Barwon River in Geelong. This resulted in Dad being interviewed on television. The adults said he gave a reasonably good interview, but all I remember was that I was excited to see Dad on TV.

Over that summer, the lagoon was rebuilt, bigger and stronger than before. I remember watching the big machinery carve out the dry ground to make a deeper dam bed and pile up the same soil to build a higher dam wall. These machines were called scrappers. They were essentially a bucket the size of a large tip truck that was dragged with its teeth pointing into the ground, to rip soil into the belly of the bucket. To empty the load, the bucket would simply be raised higher, and the contents would fall out above ground level as the machine moved along.

I think part of the reason we got to spend more time away from home was that the sheep were gone from our farm, and as beef cattle are more self-sufficient, Dad was able to be away for longer. Mum was also able to make the visits and brought us along as well. Her main motivation was to spend more time with her father, who was terminally ill with intestinal cancer. Unfortunately, I hardly remember him. He spent most of his time in his bedroom and we were not to disturb him. I do know that both of my parents had a lot of love and respect for him.

Toward the end of his time, there were moments when Mum's whole side of the family, including all of our cousins, would be staying at Wooloomanata. Sixteen grandchildren can make a lot of noise, so we were sometimes sent to the ballroom or out of the house altogether, excluding my two youngest cousins who were not deemed old enough. On one of these expulsions from the house we found the door to the storage area under the floor. It seemed as vast as the house above it, but with little light, and as it was winter, not much warmth. Fortunately, we were smart enough not to light a fire to resolve these inconveniences. Instead, some of the cousins were sent off to get a torch, while the remaining cousins, including me, explored the new territory. As our youthful eyes adjusted to the gloom, we discovered a large supply of toilet paper. This was not the most exciting of discoveries, but then my cousin David decided that they could wrap me in the toilet paper to look like a mummy and scare the others when they came back. This was agreed upon by everyone, possibly even me, and within moments I was standing with arms and legs spread and being wrapped in toilet paper with lots of gusto. So much so that within seconds they had covered my eyes, and shortly after I could hardly bend because I had been wrapped tight and many layers thick. I also had trouble talking. All these things I saw as major drawbacks, but my sisters and cousins thought it made me a more convincing mummy.

Hearing footsteps, my wrappers all hid in the dark and left me blindly facing the returning cousins as they came back with a torch. Within a few moments, they flashed their torch on me, screamed at the sight of a mummy staggering blindly toward them and ran away. Before I could be unwrapped, they brought back one of my uncles. Unfortunately, it was an uncle who lacked a sense of humour at the best of times, and this was not the best of times. He dragged me out from under the house, and still unable to detect who I was roughly ripped at the toilet paper around my face while berating me for being wasteful, insensitive, and disrespectful of my grandfather. Fortunately, one of the aunts arrived, and while she was not amused, she did at least point out that I could hardly have done it to myself. This saved me from the beating he was telling me I was about to receive.

Within months of this incident, Mum's father died in his sleep at his house in Toorak. Knowing that he was terminally ill, he had spent his final year getting his affairs in order, and part of that was arranging for each of his daughters to receive a significant inheritance. How each inheritance was used reflected the character of each daughter and their partner, and their choices would ripple through the rest of their lives. The sensible decision for my parents to make would have been to sell our farm and buy a better one. Instead, they extended the farm by purchasing neighbouring land, including Murray's, upgraded the house, and invested in our education. It was this change in fortune that put an end to my time at Haddon Primary School. We were sitting abreast on the bottom of one of the bunk beds, with our parents sitting on the single bed facing us. They told us they had some exciting news, and I think we thought we might be getting a puppy or something similar. When they said we were going to be going to a bigger, better school in Ballarat, one we had never heard of before, my memories of the school excursion to the big school came flooding back. I cried, and Cindy cried, although she often cried if someone else cried. We begged them not to make us go. Fortunately, they ignored our pleas and I started grade two at Ballarat Grammar.

It was not only the death of my grandfather that would change our farm's circumstances. A mineral processing plant, further out from Ballarat than we were, now required a constant water supply. As luck would have it, the supply pipe would run along one of the boundaries to our property, and we would be on town-water. This meant no more murky baths. Dad got a home video camera about this time, and there is footage of the first flow of town water through the garden hose, with Barb unable to control the hose due to the pressure. When you are used to the dribble of water that tank water pressure produces, these were exciting times.

The other implication of the change was that Dad needed to get back on the bulldozer. The reason for this was that some of our land, and all of Murray's, had been purchased under a government scheme to convert bushland to farmland. The land was relatively cheap, but it was a requirement that 80% of it be cleared of trees and turned into agricultural land. My parents had completed this task for our land, but a significant amount of the land they purchased from Murray still needed to be cleared.

To give Dad more time on the dozer, he hired some of the young local men, Daryl and Morris, to do the regular farm work. I recall I was helping them feed out the hay when we noticed Dad struggle to bulldoze a larger tree and stopped to watch. Our bulldozer was red and not that big, and it did not have any overhead protection for the driver. In preparing to push over a tree, the driver would remove the soil and roots around the tree, then raise the blade and push it over. The issue with this tree, was that it was not falling over on the push, instead it was falling towards the dozer as the dozer backed away. We watched this happen two or three times in a row, much to Daryl and Morris's amusement, before Dad stopped the dozer and we went over to him. After some discussion about possible alternatives, it was decided a bigger dozer was required.

Fortunately, one of the other locals, also named Bob, had a bigger dozer. He was also a bigger Bob, the only person I remember as a child being larger than my Dad. We had a Toyota Landcruiser ute, which had a handrail on the passenger side, and as kids all four of us could keep at least one hand on the rail at the same time. When big Bob put one hand on the rail, there was no room left for my hand. His fingers were thicker than a fat sausage, and his voice was at such a low rumble you would need a sub-woofer to replay it correctly. Not that he said very much. I recall being there when he came to look at the stuck dozer, and after walking around the scene in silence, he simply said, 'Give me an hour to get here, then we should have it off in about 15 minutes, and an hour to get back home – two-and-a-half hours tops.' This was apparently the quote for the work. There was an exchange of nods, and we drove big Bob back to his house and returned to the tree waiting for him to drive his dozer there.

When he did arrive, he dug out the other side of the tree a little more, put a cable around the tree and then with some distance on the cable pulled the tree as Dad pushed it. It was all over quickly. It also led to big Bob and his big dozer being hired to help Dad clear the remaining land – over 200 acres of trees. It was the part of the farm that was furthest from the house and even after it was cleared, we referred to it as the bush block. I don't recall seeing much of the actual dozing work, I think that was considered too dangerous for us. However, we did spend a lot of time picking up after it during the school holidays.

This involved Dad driving slowly forward while the kids, the four of us and a friend each, walked next to or behind the tip trailer that was towed behind the tractor. We would pick up any sticks and roots and throw them onto the trailer. Occasionally if we found something bigger, we would call out and Dad would get down and pick the stump or log up and hurl it on to the trailer. We would do this all day, for days on end. Other than stopping for morning and afternoon tea and a lunch break around a fire, the only other break we had was with the emptying of each load, when we would scramble up to the top of the elevated tray and slide down it. We and our friends enjoyed this enough to not mind the work in between. We also enjoyed each other's company and the general banter distracted from the task at hand.

My chosen friend on nearly every school holiday was Tony. We became best friends in my first year at Ballarat Grammar in a composite class – he was in grade three and I was in grade two. Fortunately, the following year the composite class remained, just a year level higher. From grade four onwards, the classes were separated, and we hardly saw each other at school, but we spent a large chunk of every school holiday staying with each other's families. So much so that I genuinely regarded his mother as my second mother.

The most fun slides were when we had people across the whole width of the tilted tray and slid down together. The cling to the top, uncontrolled chaos of the descent and the crash landing was much more fun when shared with others. Unfortunately, this was not to last. On one of these chaotic descents, Barb's friend Dorothy did not make it to the ground. As we looked up from our crashed heap of tangled bodies, we saw Dorothy was attached to the edge of the tray by an unseen force, her arms and legs flailing wildly, pleading for someone to get her down. It turned out the hooks used to keep the tailgate in place had caught on the back of her overalls. She was unharmed, but it was a close enough call to make a new rule – we were only allowed to slide down the edges, away from the hooks.

I am not sure over what time span we did the clearing up, but Dad was insistent that when it came to the night where the long rows of pushed over trees and scrub and trailer loads of picked up wood were going to be burned, that all those who helped had to be there. It was his way of saying thanks. The day itself was cold and wet, although I don't remember it raining, but I think it was picked as a time when it was unlikely that any of the surrounding bush or farmland would catch fire from a flying cinder.

At that point in time, we were too young to be involved in the actual burning, so we set up camp where we had a good view over the rows of timber and watched as they were set alight and the fire spread up each row. I remember we stayed well into the night as the fires burnt on and became beds of burning coals hundreds of metres long that stretched across the dark ground and made the surrounding trees glow. We walked around them, and by this point in the night there was no need to tell us not to get too close; the heat was so intense we would not have wanted to go closer than 20 metres.

Fire and Fireworks

Fire was such a regular part of life for most of my childhood I could not accurately place most of the following fire events into a time sequence. The fireworks on the other hand are a little easier to place.

My first memory of fireworks was at the end of grade two. My best friend Tony and I were invited to another boy's house for a Guy Fawkes Night bonfire. Guy Fawkes Night was apparently a celebration of an attempt to blow up the British Parliament and occurred in early November each year. It made no sense to me, but it did mean that we got to play with fireworks. We were each given two dozen of the smallest firecrackers to light for ourselves. I recall them being like miniature sticks of dynamite. The night itself seemed very chaotic, with older kids throwing firecrackers into the bonfire, fireworks lighting up the sky, and the bonfire being extremely hot. One kid hurt his hand when he forgot to let go of a large firecracker before it exploded. Firework related injuries were reasonably common.

The only other Guy Fawkes Night I went to was at home, shortly after the start of the house being renovated. The large cypress tree that had been in the horse paddock had been knocked over and dragged into a nearby paddock, to be burnt on Guy Fawkes Night some weeks later. Mum, sensibly, did not think that kids should have fireworks, so we were limited to watching a reasonable display of fireworks be released by the adults. The other big difference between this night and the other, was the cold. We happened to do this on the coldest November night on record, it got to minus seven degrees Celsius. It was something we were not prepared for – it had been a nice day with a clear sky and we started the night in summer clothes, then gradually added more layers and crept closer to the bonfire as the night wore on.

Firecrackers were banned soon after this, but skyrockets and other fireworks designed for the sky were still available for sale until at least year 10 – which would have been 1981. I know this because one of the kids who went home with holes burnt into his jumper from a firework shootout only arrived at the school in year 10. I was not involved in that incident, but it did involve a number of my friends, mostly boarders at the school, who had created two teams, and were using what we called ten shots (a tube of fireworks designed to be pushed into the ground, that when lit would shoot ten coloured balls of fireworks into the sky). The firework shootout involved these being lit and carried in hand and pointed at those on the other team. The tubes themselves got hot and sometimes exploded, and so it was a dangerous game for both the shooter and those being shot at – one I personally never played.

The closest I came was a few years earlier, firing small skyrockets out of coke bottles at my friend Tony, and he at me in return, at about 30 metres apart. We only had one session of it, about a dozen shots each, before deciding that the risk and reward were out of balance.

The risk and reward of fire was part of my childhood. From a young age I was responsible for keeping the fires going in the house. As fires were our only source of heating, and it gets very cold in Ballarat in winter, this was not a small task. The job included every part of the process, cleaning out the ash, lighting each fire, keeping them burning and ensuring they would die down safely around bedtime. When the house was full, we had three fires to keep alight, two open fires and one combustion heater, and we would burn about a tonne of wood a week. Part of my job required getting the right mix of wood from the wood heap, including splitting it. At first I helped to throw the cut wood onto the tip trailer, and as I got older I used the chain saw to cut down dead trees and saw them into pieces.

As the fires were the only source of heat for our house, I used to get annoyed at anyone who stood in front of the fire. In particular, I used to get annoyed at Mum, who would arrive home from work and hold out the back of her skirts to bare the back of her legs to the fire. In the process her skirts would block the heat from the whole room. My solution was to make the fire so hot that nobody could stand there for long.

The other job I was given from a young age was to light the tip. To put this in context, in the 1970s most houses had an incinerator somewhere in the yard where they burnt garden waste and other things. On farms, there was a tip – some out of the way part of the farm that could not be seen or smelt from the house, where waste was dumped and then burnt at irregular intervals.

Our tip was located on the edge of one of the disused open-cut mines on the farm, it was a steep descent. Various farm and household rubbish would be dumped onto it and then when it was deemed likely to burn, but not burn the land around it, it would be lit. The household waste was much the same as any other household – but completely unsorted. The farm waste varied with the time of year, including dead calves in calving season (autumn), hay covered string during the colder months, and left-over packaging from fertiliser, seeds and various chemicals at other times. Lighting it involved climbing down to the bottom of the pile of rubbish, finding something flammable, setting it on fire, then climbing back out again. It would not pass any occupational health and safety standard, ever. The mine wall itself was close to vertical, and hundreds of old cars had been dumped into the mine – judging by their models, in the 1940s and '50s. Our rubbish was dumped on top of them, so climbing up and down meant climbing over old car bodies, which were sometimes obscured by our rubbish.

Given that this was Australia, the tip could not be lit for most of summer, so by autumn it was a large, smelly, rodent ridden pile and very flammable. Getting to the bottom of that, lighting it, and getting out before the fire took hold was always an adrenaline filled experience. Particularly if the lower rubbish included aerosol cans, which would explode and fly off in random directions.

But this was not my most stressful encounter with fire. That would come from fighting bushfires as part of the Country Fire Authority

(CFA), which I will talk about later, but the other was lighting what we called gorse bushes.

Gorse bushes were native to Scotland and were introduced to Australia by Scottish miners wanting a reminder of home. They were green, prickly, and had a yellow flower. In Australia, and particularly around us, they had become a noxious weed. They grew into impenetrable bushes two metres tall and clumped together in vast thickets. Large tracts of our farm were infested with them, particularly along the creek, so much so that most of the creek was unreachable.

Farmers are required by law to remove noxious weeds from their properties. This was originally done using plant killers, including DTD. When these were banned, or when the gorse thickets were so vast that spraying was impractical, the bushes were burnt. Gorse bushes are initially difficult to light, but once alight turn into a furnace, this is apparently because they are full of a very flammable oil. I say furnace without any exaggeration – I have seen flames twelve metres high.

We set fire to them by using the same firelighters that firefighters use to create back-burns in the bush. This involves a hand-held fuel can, with a long neck leading to a fire-head that drips the burning fuel onto the ground or anything it touches. Given my relative comfort with and understanding of fire, I was regarded as being responsible enough to be one of the firelighters when I was still in primary school.

For the most part it is not that exciting, because the fire takes a few minutes to take hold, the experience is generally a long walk next to prickly bushes, trying to push a lit stick as far under the bushes as possible so that it can catch onto the drier, older parts of the plant. My sisters, who would come along and watch, had a much more interesting time because they got to see the fire take hold and the rabbits running away from it. The monotony of the fire lighting role can also be disorientating.

One time when we were burning the gorse along the creek, I was lighting one side, and Dad the other. The creek was not a straight line, and the width of the bushes also varied, so that as we walked along, we would wind together and apart. We had been doing this for at least on hour, when I looked ahead of me to see the gorse already ablaze and the rabbits sprinting all around me. My initial thought was that Dad had got ahead of me on the other side of the creek, and that the fire had jumped across the creek. But I was wrong, I had been so focused on the task at hand that I had headed into a clearing and had inadvertently surrounded myself in fire. I dropped the fire lighter and sprinted with the fleeing rabbits for the small gap between the walls of flame. A few moments later I heard the fire lighter explode. A few moments later Dad came bursting through to our side of the creek badly scratched from the gorse to check that we were all okay. From then on I was always very careful to pay more attention to what was going on around me when we were lighting the gorse bushes.

It was the start of February, the end of summer in Australia, when the vegetation is dry, and the air is hot. I was in late primary school, and I had bought my sister Barb an ant-farm for her birthday – problem was, it had no ants. I knew where there was a large bull-ant nest on the farm. Because it was going to be a surprise, I said that I was going to the fishing hole to check on how the local teacher was doing (he had driven past the house five minutes earlier). So, I set off on Cindy's bike with a shovel, an ice cream container, some paper and a few matches in the parcel rack on the back. My plan was to use the lit paper to make the ants go underground (similar to using smoke to calm a beehive), then use the shovel to dump some of them into the container, seal the lid, put out what was left of the lit paper and go home to give Barb an ant-filled ant farm. Unfortunately, things did not go to plan.

Things started out well enough, the screwed-up roll of burning paper on top of the ant nest did make them go underground – and as there was no vegetation on the ant nest, it was not burning anything else. So, I started digging. Unfortunately, my digging continually resulted in shovelfuls of dirt without ants in them. It was also upsetting the ants. I moved where I was digging a few times, and then realised that something else was on fire. It was the grass next to the nest. I tried putting it out with the shovel, tried throwing dirt on it, but it was getting bigger. Realising it was now out of my control, I jumped on the bike and headed for home to raise the alarm.

At this time, Haddon did not have its own fire brigade, so by the time the fire trucks arrived from nearby districts, the fire had spread – in the end it burnt around 20 acres. As was traditional, after the fire was out, my parents invited all those who had helped to stay for a beer. At least one of them asked which one of us kids had started the fire, my sisters said very strongly that it wasn't any of us and that I had seen it going somewhere else and reported it. My sisters sounded very convincing, so I made myself scarce as I have never been particularly good at lying.

Later that night, after everyone else had gone and my sisters were in bed, my parents got me to go to their room. They told me that they knew I had lit the fire because I had left the gate open, so could not have been going to the water hole. I admitted that it was me, and told them what had happened, accompanied by tears and sobs. In a way I was relieved to tell the truth. My punishment was that I had to tell the truth to anyone who asked. I accepted this with absolute commitment that I would do so, even though it filled me with dread – I would have much preferred a few rounds of the wooden spoon. Being known for lighting fires in country Australia was the worst sort of reputation to have.

As a family, I cannot recall going to church outside of weddings, funerals, and christenings. That night I prayed very earnestly that no one would ask me about the fire. Nobody did ask, for which I was extremely grateful and have believed in God, although not always religion, ever since.

The threat of fires is one of the things that unites country communities. Everyone knows that when they, their homes, families, farms, and livestock are threatened by the raging monster that is an out-of-control fire in the Australian summer, they need to rely on each other. This can help put perspective into lots of other little issues that could otherwise fracture a collection of people with little in common other than location.

Unfortunately, it was another tragic event that brought the Haddon community together. A boy was abducted into a car while walking home from the Haddon primary school. His family had only moved into the district a year earlier, and as we had left the primary school a year before that, I did not know the boy at all. I do remember the search for him.

Most of the local kids were at our house, where one of Mum's school friends that we affectionately called Aunt Sal, (Aunt Sal had driven up from Melbourne to provide what help she could), was given the task of keeping us distracted while our parents were searching the district for a child who had now been missing overnight.

Sal was a big jovial personality who was immensely popular with kids. I am not sure of the series of events, but somehow it was decided that we would all dress up in strange costumes – and then go on a picnic. I suspect that this was a combination of ideas that would take a long time to execute and keep us distracted and physically active at the same time.

The missing boy lived two km to the east of the school on the way to Ballarat, and the car that had taken him had last been seen heading in that direction. So, most of the search was also in that direction. Sal took all of us, through our paddocks in the other direction. Some kids were wearing old lamp shades as hats, and other strange combinations of clothes. Each of us carried part of the picnic, and Sal ensured we all stayed together – although we spread out like Brown's cows.

One of the passing media crews spotted us from the road and rushed over to get some footage thinking that we were part of the search. Sal made us stay where we were and went over and talked to them out of earshot. I recall watching her, in fancy costume herself, very strenuously telling them to go away. Apparently, she had to explain several times that we were not part of the search before they agreed not to use the footage. It would have been a very strange looking search party if they had.

The boy's body was found a few days later, and his murderer captured and convicted.   But it permanently changed the neighbourhood. We were all told numerous times not to walk on the roads alone, nor to accept lifts with strangers. After knowing what happened, none of us needed to be told – but I think the parents needed to tell us. Also, any passing neighbour would ask kids if they wanted a lift home. As kids, we adapted. The roads were never that busy and we could usually hear a car coming before it came into view, so we got in the habit of hiding whenever we knew a car was coming.

The other thing that changed the neighbourhood was a continuous influx of people. Referred to as hobby farmers, these were usually young families with parents who worked in Ballarat. They generally had five to 10 acres of land – which the farmers joked was too much to mow but not enough to farm. The family who lost their son were one of the first of the hobby farmer families.

Another of the new arrivals was the Cobbs. They were English immigrants, with a girl my age and twin boys Cindy's age. They got along very well with my parents, which meant that our families often spent time together. They also owned pigs. One summer evening our families got together for a meal and drinks. The meal over, but with plenty of daylight left, the kids decided to play hide and seek in the paddock between the house and pig stye. The grass was waist height for an adult, so close to head height for me. One of the parents called out that we needed to watch out for snakes. I remember the instruction and the impossibility of following it, the grass was so thick, even where it had been flattened, that there was no chance of seeing a snake even a few centimetres away.

This observation inspired me to change my tactics. Rather than lying still in the long grass hoping not to be discovered, I moved along the paths of flattened grass hoping to see the person early enough to run away from them. The trick in these games is when being pursued to run towards others so that the pursuer gets distracted. We played multiple rounds of this game, and the sun got lower in the sky, so that the shadows across the grass were longer, darker, and harder to read. Eventually, I was spotted and pursued. I sprinted along the track in the other direction. My bare feet, pounding on the flattened grass paths, detected that the ground was getting damper. I glanced back over my shoulder at my pursuer as I went around a corner and slammed straight into the side of a large sow who was quietly eating there. She was about my height, but at least ten times my weight, so I was repelled backwards like I had hit a wall. I was unfamiliar with pigs, and now I was lying on my back on wet ground, with an unhappy sow looming over me. She turned her head to face me, looked down her snout, snorted at me and my struggles to regain my breath and my feet. Then, she turned back to eating undeterred.

The year before the boy went missing, my sister Debbie and I stayed with another of the earliest hobby farmers. The parents were also immigrants. Their childhood had been in Holland during the Second World War, and they were hoping to create a better life for their kids. The father still used English as a second language. They had a girl and then three boys. The girl Jacquie was the same age as my oldest sister Deb and the two of them would become close friends. I was the same age as the middle boy. It would be a visit that would give me a change in perspective.

It was shortly after Christmas, and the topic of presents was raised. It was the first Christmas after my grandfather had died, and Mum had been very generous. I had been given a train set and a cowboy and Indian set that included tepee and a fort, as well as a Santa sack of other presents. The three boys had been given the exact same cowboy and Indian set – to share between the three of them, and no other presents. It was taken out and shared with such reverence that I felt guilty and stayed silent about having one myself.

The other things I remember from the visit was that they only had three cows, two of which had gotten out because the fences were in disrepair. We went looking for them in the bush behind their property, which we did in the family car – a Volkswagen Beetle. I remember being surprised that the engine was in the boot and very noisy. It also made me realise that they did not have any other farm vehicles or equipment. I had become aware that we were the poorer family among my cousins, I now realised that we were the richer family among the neighbours.

The following day was also eventful – the youngest boy, "Freddy" (not his real name), got attacked by a magpie – it landed on his head and pulled out a chunk of hair with its beak leaving a hole with blood spurting out. Freddy wore an ice cream container on his head for the rest of the day. I have never seen a magpie do that to anyone else since, but I am still wary of magpies.

I did not return the visit invite because I was embarrassed about how many toys I had in comparison. Then I went to a different school and so did not spend time with the boys after that. Although a few years later, when they were high school age, I did see them on the school bus and we exchanged friendly nods, but we got on at different stops and never sat together.

For Richer or Poorer

Placing events in time can be challenging. I swapped schools at the start of grade two, which would be February 1973, Gough Whitlam would be famously sacked as prime minister at the end of 1975 and in between those two events my parents would go from richer to poorer.

The increase in wealth would have started sometime in 1972, but as a six year old I did not notice it until Christmas. The expansion of the farm to more than twice its size was not noticeable to me, as Dad had been managing the other farm anyway and so who owned it was not relevant. This was particularly true as part of the arrangement was that Murray (usually accompanied by his friend Len) was still welcome to visit the property to go rabbit shooting. It seemed that this was all he really wanted the property for in the first place.

I imagine that as a high-profile individual it would have been a very welcome escape to wander around with a good friend in absolute privacy. I say wander around, because in all the times I came across them in well over a decade I never saw any evidence that they shot a rabbit. They carried rifles, and they walked long distances, but they tended to go to the more scenic parts of the property rather than where the rabbits were more commonly found. Also, any time we came across them they were happy to chat.

Murray was good with words. He made the everyday entertaining and had the gift of putting people at ease. Len was the quieter of the two, happy to talk when given a chance, but more often restricted to smiles and nods as Murray rolled out the jokes and stories. A standard joke from Murray was how my sisters and I never wore shoes.

This was largely true. On the farm we either wore bare feet or gumboots. This started from when we were young, and our games merged the inside and the outside of our little house. The rule was that we had to take off our shoes to come inside. So, we decided not to wear the shoes, and as we were not allowed to wear socks outside, bare feet were the natural solution. I think the rules were an attempt to keep the dirt out of the house, and stop the socks being wrecked. While it saved the socks, I am not sure about the dirt: our feet were tough and often dark with worn-in grit. We could walk and run on gravel roads baked by the summer sun without flinching. Much to Mum's frustration, we could neither clean nor remove our feet when entering the house.

The house was the most conspicuous indication of our change in fortune. It would more than triple in size, and as such we would be living in a building site for nearly two years. The house would eventually occupy all of what had been the garden around the house, possibly a little bit more. The horse paddock would become the lawn, and a few of the smaller farm sheds and water tanks would be removed. Mum would finally have a house she could be proud of.

The inspiration for the house was the front door and two metres high, one-and-a-half metres wide sash windows that had been part of Mum's parents' house in Toorak before it was demolished by the new owner. The task of designing a house around these was given to an architect (the husband of one of Mum's friends from university). I am not sure if it was for tax or sentimental reasons that the new house was to be fashioned out of the old house, because they were unrecognisable from each other.

The new house was built in three stages, the first was to extend the front, the second was to extend the back, and the third was to remove the old roof and join the two in the middle. I think it was all meant to be completed in six months – but things did not go to plan.

The first phase started on time, the old veranda (still with a big glue-patch with tyre tracks through it) was demolished and the roses and picket fence were removed to make way for the extension. The new frame was put up very quickly, and then worked stopped. The building of the house coincided with the Whitlam years, and unions were flexing their muscles – an outcome of which was we could not get bricks or tiles.

The architect proposed an alternative, second-hand slate for the roof and Mount Gambier Stone (white limestone) for the walls. Mum needed some convincing, so the whole family went to Mount Gambier in South Australia to see the stone being cut out of the quarry and sliced into slabs (much larger than a normal house brick) and various other shapes. I remember some of the workmen showing us various fossils that they had uncovered and set aside. The limestone was from an old seabed and seashells were not uncommon, and some would even be part of our walls. I have no idea what colour the original tiles and bricks were going to be, but I do know the striking white walls and dark slate roof that were to clad the house so distinctly were Plan B. One of the issues with resorting to Plan B was once a building project has started is that it opens contract renegotiations in favour of the builder. The house would cost significantly more than planned. It also took longer, the builders had to learn how to lay slate (much harder than tiles), and Mount Gambier Stone, (you can cut it to size with a carpentry saw).

As kids we were unaware of any of the finances, we just treated the changes around the house as new things to play with. As the house was being replumbed to take advantage of the town water this included lots of trenches. Most of these were dug with the Council grader – the same one used to maintain the roads. It was available for hire, with the driver, for private property. As we were putting in water troughs in a number of paddocks as well as water to the house, and septic and sewerage pipes out of the house, there were 100s of metres of 'V' shaped trenches created by the grader around the house ready for the various pipework to be put in. I have a distinct memory of this as I had two friends over to stay for the weekend, Tony and Wayne. They were both in grade three and I was in grade two in the composite class at Ballarat Grammar. It had been a relatively equitable three-way friendship up to this point, but things were about to change.

We started out playing an imaginary shooting game. Where we yelled out shots and made claims on whether someone was hit or not. As this played out, we started to use the trenches more, and with clumps of dirt in ready supply, we switched from an honesty system on who was being hit by whom, to a more evidence-based dirt throwing system (no rocks allowed). The readily available clumps of dirt would explode on impact and leave a clear mark – like paint ball. To this point it was three individual teams, and a count of ten if shot and it had all been fairly even. But when we switched to live ammunition – Tony and I were clearly out-gunned. Wayne could throw further and more accurately, he also moved and reloaded while we were counting so that we only just finished counting before being hit again from a different direction. A truce was called, and it was agreed that it would be fairer and more fun if Tony and I teamed up against Wayne. Wayne still won, but it was the start of a long friendship between Tony and me.

Wayne left the school two years later. His dad had been killed in the Vietnam War when Wayne was a baby, and his mum worked in a medical role at a low security prison some distance from Ballarat. Wayne and his sister spent the school weeks living with their paternal grandparents in Ballarat and going home on the weekends and for school holidays. I went and stayed with him on a few weekends, his house (which was his maternal grandparents' house) was like the original version of our house with a much bigger vegetable garden, and his mum and her parents were kind and gentle. Because weekends were the only time Wayne saw his mum, she was reluctant to have him stay with others, so having him come and stay at our house was a treat. The sacrifices made by Wayne's mum and his grandparents in pursuit of a good education for her children were not lost on the school, nor were they the only parents making sacrifices. I believe that while there were children of wealthy families at the school while I was there, it had a very egalitarian ethos. Even so, for those struggling to pay the school fees, it did not take much to tip the balance from difficult to impossible. In Wayne's case it was a decline in the health of his paternal grandparents that would make it impossible for him to stay at the school.

While the trenches were only around for a few weeks, the interruption to farm fences that the building works created was addressed using portable electric fences for a couple of years. These had insulated posts, not unlike a short tent pole, that an adult could push into the ground with a heavy foot. Through the insulated eye at the top of these posts ran a single wire. It was a nylon string with copper wire woven through it, orange like the poles. The wire was connected to a charger, which pulsed high voltage through it. The intent was that if livestock touched the fence, they would get a fright from the electric shock and step back from the fence. While it will never stop a stampede it generally works on grazing animals.

I was told that volts you feel, amps will kill. I learnt this was true through childhood observations. Electric fences are high voltage so you definitely feel it, but very low amps (a pulse every second or so), so that it is not going to kill. I also observed that if you are part of a chain of people and one on the end touches the fence, it is the person on the end furthest from the wire that feels it the most – particularly if you are wearing gumboots and they are not.

Farm kids enjoy seeing city kids do dumb things on farms – more for their stupefied reaction than anything else. Electric fences give great reactions. Having them so close to the house was also very convenient. We would play hide and seek outside close to dusk when the electric fences were harder to see. We would come up with reasons to walk in a line holding hands, so one of us could grab the electric fence and send a shock through to the person on the other end. But these were one-time gags, no one ever fell for it a second time. And then there was Gaynor.

Gaynor was Cindy's friend, also from Ballarat Grammar. She was a city girl, who did her best to do the farm stuff, even being one of the regulars on the clearing of the bush block and sliding down the tip trailer. However, Gaynor was always a little out of place on the farm, so likely to get herself into difficulty that we did not even try and play tricks on her. This included the electric fence. I think we even told her it was there. Somehow Gaynor managed to get her copper bangle tangled in the electric wire. I recall seeing her jolting with each electric pulse and trying to speak but being unable to. Cindy was first there and jolted along with Gaynor as she tried to untangle the wire from the bangle and Gaynor. Both were in bare feet and the ground was wet – so they were getting the full charge. I went running toward the charger to turn it off, only to find that it had been moved. Then someone pulled out a post and earthed the wire in a puddle. I think Dad had to cut the wire to get Gaynor out, and while she made light of the event, she was clearly shaken. We didn't trick anyone with electric fences after that.

Living within a building site can be difficult and hazardous, and not always in ways you would expect. At one point in the renovation the house had been extended either end, with a higher roof, so that parts of the old house that remained were within it. This included the kitchen, minus two of its walls. The state of the building meant that the temperature was the same inside and out. We were having breakfast, when Cindy and I had a disagreement about something – I really don't remember what. It escalated, she threw my beanie (woollen hat) onto the kitchen roof, I gave her a big push, causing her to land in an open box of builder's nails. She came back at me, we wrestled, my face hit the concrete slab – and broke my two front teeth. The break was the two corners in the middle such that I could close my mouth and stick a pencil through the gap. It hurt.

After much drama at home explaining what had happened to my parents, it was decided that I needed to be taken to the dentist quickly to see if he could put my teeth back together. Cindy had kindly collected the two neatly broken pieces from the concrete. We need not have rushed in, the dentist concluded that my teeth were still growing and so the repair needed to wait until I was 12, which was four years away. The school photos for the intervening years are not good.

While the house was being built, there were also a few other things that changed. One of the good ones was that we had a family holiday, for two years in a row. To put this in perspective, in my entire childhood we only had four family holidays. The first two were to the beach in January. It was to Point Lonsdale, which was where my parents had holidayed as children. They enjoyed reliving old times, and we enjoyed being at the beach.

I could not swim at all, so I spent most of the time either playing in the rockpools, jumping tiny waves, or building things out of sand. The highlight was going into the surf with Dad. He had been a particularly good swimmer and a surf lifesaver, so I was in good hands. He would take me into the breaking waves held on his hip in one arm. Then with each wave he would call under or over, and we would proceed to either launch over the wave, or have it crash over us. I loved it.

But the good times would not last. The economics of farming were being rewritten. Australia is generally not blessed with good soil, and so farmers invest in improving the soil. This involves ploughing, fertilising, crop rotations and stock management. The first three of these involve a lot of energy, which requires fuel. With the advent of the worldwide oil price shock in 1973, the cost of improving farmland skyrocketed. Other significant farm costs like debt finance (interest rates), labour, transport and machinery were also increasing significantly, while farm income from wool and meat were stagnant or in decline.

Our farm had poor soil, in part because there had been three major gold mining operations on it where the debris and quartz (seams of rock in which gold might be found) were broken up and dumped on ground nearby. The quartz was valued by the miners and so was usually discarded in a collection colloquially called a mullock heap. The rest of the debris was treated as an inconvenience and spread around. It made terrible topsoil. There were sections of the farm where this was so prevalent that we did not even bother clearing the trees.

While Mum had inherited a significant amount of money, the cost of extending and improving the farm and the house were more than she had inherited, and so the size of the bank loan had also increased. I don't know the specifics of the finances, but I do recall Mum visiting the bank after school. We all waited in the car for what seemed like a long time, until she eventually reappeared visibly upset. When we asked her what was wrong, she said that they were crooks who had changed the rules and that we would be changing banks. As kids, this just meant we would be parking somewhere else next time she went to the bank, but I think for Mum that signalled the end of her dream.

The change in finances hit us kids just before the federal election, after the Whitlam government was sacked. The family got a colour TV, but it was paid for by the inheritance that had been put aside for each of us by Dad's aunt. I was familiar with colour TV because Tony's family owned one the entire time I knew him, they also got Melbourne TV, in addition to Ballarat TV, which meant five channels instead of two. I assumed that we would also be getting extra channels because of this and was disappointed when we still only had the local BTV6 and the ABC. I was also unhappy about spending the inheritance on a shared TV – I think I was saving up for something. But my sisters glared at me, and the fact that it was already a done deal made me put up and shut up.

The reason I know we had it in time for the election, was that the election results was one of the first things we watched where the colour added meaning. Although my understanding of seats in parliament was a bit lacking, I had been to my first VFL (now AFL) Grand Final a few months earlier, and I thought seats in parliament were allocated on a similar basis. I remember thinking that they should have just queued up earlier or saved up and paid extra if they really wanted to get the 'key seats'.

In Sickness and in Health

Like most farm kids in the '70s we were generally in robust good health. Childhood obesity was rare, not because we had good diets (we didn't), but because we were physically active at every opportunity.

Our diet was generally high in fat and sugar. We had full cream milk, as well as cream and a coating of sugar on our cereal. Most of the cake and biscuit recipes had almost equal quantities of sugar and flour, some recipes even required lard – which is animal fat. Our diets generally had substantial doses of animal fat in most things as it was considered flavoursome. Chops and steaks were served with a thick rim of fat. Roasts were cooked with the fat on, and any fat that melted away would be captured in the gravy to be poured over the meal.

We always had dessert after the evening meal, and almost regardless of the dessert we had the option of adding cream and/or ice cream as an accompaniment – as casually as people are offered salt and pepper with a savoury meal. If ice cream was the feature dish for dessert, then we would be given a choice of flavoured toppings (chocolate, strawberry and caramel being the staple range).

The focus of every meal was the meat, which was always plentiful. The vegetables and salad were just add-ons. Salads were either very dull or full of unhealthy additions. The dull version was lettuce with chunks of tomato. There was only one kind of lettuce – iceberg. The fancier version of the salad included one or more of the following additions: cubes of cheese, beetroot, grated carrot, slices of cucumber and salad dressing.

If we had guests then there would also be nibbles, again these were simple. Bags of potato chips and peanuts emptied into bowls, and flat plates with cubes of cheese and slices of cabana (spiced sausage) skewered by tooth-picks. But like the salad, these were just an accompaniment to the drinks, which, like the meat, was plentiful. For adults, drink driving was not yet a phrase, let alone a consideration, and the ability to consume vast quantities of alcohol was respected. Hosting was a whole family responsibility, and so as kids we would not only hand around the nibbles, but also mix the drinks. Mum's favourite drink was a brandy and dry on ice, and I could create that to her liking from early primary school. Like everything else on the farm, the alcohol and mixers were purchased in bulk, and as we got older, we would try various alcoholic drinks without our parents' knowledge. Fortunately for our health, we did not really like the taste.

As kids, we did not drink much soft drink at home. However, full cream milkshakes with rich doses of vanilla ice cream and flavoured topping were commonplace throughout the warmer months. There were no 'diet' varieties of any of these foods. With an oversupply of milk, we drank milkshakes in large quantities. So much so that my sisters often referred to my bloated belly as a 'milkpot' – but the rest of me remained very lean, which could be problematic in winter.

On at least two occasions as a young child, I got so cold while out and about that we stopped the tractor and trailer, found shelter, and started a fire so that we could warm up. As most adults smoked there was never any problem finding matches or a cigarette lighter, and the middle of the hay bales would be dry enough to help get a fire started. Second-hand smoke was also omni-present in our childhood, some teachers even smoked in the classroom. While Mum didn't smoke, Dad did, and to ensure that a cigarette was readily available he had a packet of cigarettes in most of the vehicles and various rooms in the house. This made it very easy for us to pinch smokes from him and try smoking ourselves. Cindy nearly vomited the first time and never tried it again. Deb and I smoked for about three months, even supplying some of our friends with cigarettes. The increase in cigarette consumption caused Dad some concern, resulting in him quitting. Part of this process was to swap cigarettes for chewing gum, which he distributed around the house and vehicles in a similar way.

The approach to diet, smoking and drinking were not the only things very different to today. There was also a very different attitude to diseases. I cannot imagine that lockdowns would have even been contemplated if COVID had occurred in the '70s, given the approach taken to other diseases that were relatively mild on the young and much harsher and possibly deadly on the elderly.

I remember going to a chickenpox party at a neighbour's house. Their children had caught chickenpox and so, while they were still infectious, other children in the neighbourhood without immunity were invited around to catch it. The idea was that the younger we were exposed, the better we would be able to deal with it and establish life-long immunity. The party achieved its aim, and in the following weeks I recall the four of us standing in a circle in the bathroom applying calamine lotion to the back of the person in front of us. We were young enough that my older sisters were not concerned about being topless.

I also remember when Cindy got the mumps. Her face swelled up massively so that she had a moon-face, and she was clearly uncomfortable. So, I was not very happy to be told that this was a great opportunity for me to get the mumps before puberty. I spent the next week sharing her cups and cutlery to maximise my exposure, and fortunately got a very mild version of it.

Not all diseases were given the same treatment. There was a distinct difference in attitude between measles and German measles. Anyone with the possibility of having German measles (rubella) would self-isolate, particularly from women that might be of childbearing age. Word would spread so that women who were pregnant could also isolate themselves. These precautions were to prevent the unborn child from getting rubella. It was not a fool-proof system and there were a few children at Ballarat Grammar that were 'rubella kids'.

There were also some kids at Grammar that were 'thalidomide kids' in the years above me. Thalidomide is a drug that was marketed as a sedative and treatment for morning sickness in pregnant women in the late '50s and early '60s. This drug subsequently caused babies to be born with a range of disabilities. The most obvious ones were missing or shrunken limbs, with hands appearing to be attached directly to shoulders, and legs not extending beyond the edge of the seat of a wheelchair, but there were also less dramatic ones. In the year above me there was a kid with a club foot, and partial deafness.

The slow awareness of the thalidomide side-effects created some distrust of the medical profession. However, the family doctor was still given an elevated status in all medical decisions. Meanwhile the long-term impact of chemicals and products widely used over the previous two decades was starting to be revealed. For many years after smoking was widely acknowledged as carcinogenic, cigarette advertising was still a dominant feature of sports sponsorship and television and newspaper advertising. On farms products like DDT were being sold at heavy discounts in the lead up to being banned and were stockpiled for use in later years. Chemicals were also applied to animals, drenches were squirted down their throats for worms, lice and tick treatments were applied to their skin, and some farms also injected hormones.

Skin cancer was also not on anyone's radar. A suntan was considered a sign of health, and many a pale skinned person was scorched red trying to get one. I spent most summers without a shirt on.   Sunburnt shoulders, noses and cracked lips were commonplace among my family and friends. As were gravel rashes on knees – the occupational hazard of riding bikes on gravel and playing tennis on bitumen.

Riding and Cattle Work

We were made to feel useful from an early age. Whatever work was being undertaken on the farm would be tackled as a team, with each of us having something to do. I realised years later that much of this task allocation was for our benefit. My sisters and I have all grown up with a decent work ethic and a strong sense of team. Despite being four quite different individuals, we have also been resilient with healthy self-esteem. The farm work from which we got the strongest sense of teamwork was what we called 'cattle work'.

The main cattle work happened three times a year, with the key task being related to where the cows were in the annual breeding cycle. These tasks included pregnancy testing, early calving and weaning. On our farm they lined up with school holidays, and each process lasted about a week. Our days started with getting the horses ready and loading the Landcruiser with the necessary equipment. Then we would round up the nominated cattle from one of the paddocks and herd them to the cattle yards. Once in the yards, we would separate the cows from the calves, and then process each animal through the crush. At the end of the day, we would herd them back – usually to a different paddock.

While Debbie was still in primary school, Mum was part of the cattle work team, but after that she only participated occasionally. This was because by then we had all the roles covered, particularly as we generally had a friend each, with Dad included made a team of nine. Tasks were allocated by a combination of ability and interest, and while there was some bargaining, I don't recall any arguments.

We had three horses of different sizes. Initially it was Max, Prince and Trigger – all were geldings. Max was bred and trained as a polo horse. He was large, quick, agile and headstrong. He had a black coat with a splash of white on his nose. Prince was a medium sized horse, with a gentle temperament. He was chestnut in colour with white socks and a white stripe on his face. Trigger was smaller, as he was a pony. He looked like a smaller version of Prince, but behaved like a smaller version of Max.

One of Trigger's characteristics was that he was keen on being home. If we were within two paddocks of the house, he would do what he could to get there quickly. On the way out this involved rearing up and trying to throw off the rider, on the way home it involved a flat-out sprint without much thought about whether the gate was open or shut. It became my job to ride Trigger until he was far enough away from the house that he would forget about going home.

Once the thoughts of home had passed from his mind Trigger was a pleasant, although a little lazy, horse, happily ridden by lots of our friends. Horse riding on the farm, while not disagreeable, was never done for pleasure. It was always with a task in mind, usually the cattle work, occasionally to bring in a cow having trouble calving, or to take a bull back to the paddock he had escaped from. The horses knew the routine as well as we did which generally made them an easy ride for the uninitiated. Trigger would eventually be replaced by Sam, a genuine stock horse. He was middle sized, barrel chested, and most importantly had been trained to have excellent stock sense. I recall a university friend of mine, who rode horses with all the elegance of a sack of potatoes, falling off Sam while chasing a cow that had broken from the herd. While my friend was collecting himself and his thoughts, Sam rounded up the cow and returned it to the herd before going back to collect my friend.

Max would never have done that. Max tested his rider, and if he found you wanting you were in for an unpleasant time in the saddle. Indeed, Max tested people when they were trying to saddle him or clean his hooves as well. My cousin Sarah was the first person to ride Max other than Dad. Sarah had a no-nonsense approach to life; she gave no nonsense, and she took no nonsense. She was grounded and accustomed to dealing with her father's polo horses. So, when Max tried to bite her while she was in the process of brushing him, she instinctively met his nose with her elbow and gained the brute's respect.

As we got older my sister Cindy would be the next to ride Max. Cindy sat well in the saddle and, to my knowledge, was never thrown. Smaller in stature and gentler in temperament, she took a different approach to getting Max's obedience. Recognising that he was keen on a fight, she gave him a very loose rein until he quickly ran out of ideas. Once he was bored, she took up the reins again and was forever in control.

Chasing errant cattle on horseback can be exhilarating. Chasing them through trees or over rough ground was even more so. You learn to trust the horse with experience because, unlike a car, it can think and navigate its own way through obstacles. What they don't always judge correctly is height. I recall chasing a young bull through some trees on Sam. Several clumps of leaves had already brushed across me, so I was leaning down over his neck when I saw the branch. I dropped as low as I could go, but still struck the wood with the top of my helmet. Fortunately, the branch broke, rather than me.

Dad was not so lucky. Although he did not hit a branch, his horse was tossed by a bull. He was on Max chasing the bull across a paddock when the bull turned and put its head under the front shoulder of the horse and lifted it off its feet. Dad was still in the saddle when they landed, so that he was partially crushed by the horse. Fortunately, nothing was broken, and both Dad and Max recovered – although Dad did spend a few weeks healing, during which he would proudly show us and any visitors his extensive bruises.

But these incidents were rare. Generally, the horse ride was a gentle stroll to the relevant paddock, with a casual chat between the riders. This was always punctuated by intermittent catch-up trots from the smaller horses. It was the bit I disliked about having the smaller horse. The larger horse just had a casual walk, while the smaller horse would trot out to be in front, only to be slowly over-taken and then do it all again. I never liked trotting so to me this was annoying. We did also canter and gallop at various points, but only if there was time and space to calm the horses again before we engaged with the cattle. This helped to keep the cattle calm.

While the horses were heading for the cattle, the person driving the Landcruiser ute was going to the cattle yards. There they would set up the gates and unload the various items that were going to be used in the yards. This would include the drenching equipment for squirting worm medicine into their mouths; anti-lice equipment for squirting a liquid medicine on their backs, horn, hoof and hair clippers, and so forth. In essence, a visit to the yards for the cattle was both a manicure and a medical check-up and sometimes involved the veterinarian.

Once the yards were set up – with one side open to receive the cattle from the direction they were coming – the driver would go towards the cattle ensuring that the path was clear, and all gates were open along the way. When on horseback it was easy to hear the vehicle approach as it was a constant din of rattling metal. There were several reasons for this. One was that it was an old vehicle and so various bolts and bits had been replaced by fence wire and spare bits of metal. But mostly it was because it always carried some fencing equipment, a coil of wire and an old army ammunitions tin complete with lid, that was full of tools used to repair a fence. They rattled and crashed like a falling set of percussion instruments over every bump, and on the farm the bumps were plentiful.

The Landcruiser also carried the rest of the crew. If we each had a friend that meant six people, which would be a maximum of three in the cabin and the rest on the back, with those on the back either standing up looking over the cabin or sitting on the fencing box. When it wasn't raining the back was more popular as sitting in the front meant you had to open the gates.

Once the cattle had been herded together, the Landcruiser rattled along at the back, while the horses were on one side, with a fence along the other. Generally being at the back was easiest, so the person riding Max, usually Dad, would be closest to the front. The horse at the front was required to discourage the front of the herd from bolting, as well as being ready to squeeze through the gate with the herd so that they could race out and round up any breakaways back to the fence and the rest of the herd. None of the cattle could outrun or outmanoeuvre Max, and Max seemed to enjoy chasing them down and wheeling them in.

Once the cattle were contained in the yards, the horses would be loosely tethered in the shade of some nearby trees, and we would begin the yard work. This generally involved the whole crew, although some friends were more reluctant than others to walk among the herd with only a length of black plastic piping for protection. The pipe was an off cut from irrigation pipe about the width of a tennis racket handle.

The first job was to separate the calves from the cows. To do this we would have someone guard a gate between the two yards, usually Dad, while the rest of us would walk through the herd to find the calves. This was harder when we were younger as we could not see over the cows, so it was like a game of hide and seek, particularly because the cows wanted their calves with them. But our constant movement through the herd stirred them like a spoon through a sauce in a pot, so that calves were often found in clumps at the edges. We would then push the calves forward toward the gate, the guard would step aside to let them through while blocking any cows that tried to get through with them.

Once we had separated the cows from the calves, we generally had a break for morning tea, which also allowed the calves and cows to settle into the separation. We then processed either the cows or the calves depending on the agenda for the day. For example, if it was pregnancy testing, then we adjusted for when the vet was due to arrive. If it was weaning, we did the calves first, so we knew which cows were going to be separated off to be sent to market.

Farming is a business, and beef farming is about converting pasture into quality meat. As our farm did not have high quality pasture, the herd needed to be actively managed. The cattle work was the application of this management. Part of this was understanding that poor quality cattle eat the same amount as good quality cattle, so improving the quality of the cattle improved the productivity of the farm. This was done through proactive selection of the breeding stock. While each calf had two parents, a cow only had one calf per year, while the bull sired thirty or more calves per year. So, investing in good bulls was a good way to improve the quality of the herd.

With the cows it was more clinical. On our farm, the cows calved in autumn, got pregnant in winter, were weaned off the calves in summer, and then the cycle repeated. If at any point they did not have a calf, or were about to have a calf – they were sold. The quality of the offspring was also a factor. Every year the best 30 heifers (female calves) were kept, and a similar number of cows were sold, keeping the overall breeding herd at around 150 – five mobs of 30. As one of those mobs contained the next generation of heifers, we produced around 120 calves a year. With the gender split roughly 50:50, it meant that half the heifers were also sold every year, usually as breeding stock to other farmers.

For the male calves, the ratio was not so good. In the early days we sold all of them as yearling (less than a year old) steers (bulls with their testicles removed at least a few months earlier). Then the quality of the herd improved to a point when we were able to breed our own bulls as well as sell them for a premium price to other beef farmers. Even then about 80% of the males were sold as yearling steers. What made a dramatic difference to the quality of the herd was the use of computers.

When we first started beef farming, the quality of the herd was managed largely based on a visual assessment. Also, the calves were not tagged, so the assessment and the notes had to be made while the cows and calves were in the field. Then things got more scientific. A university in Tamworth in NSW created a computer program that assessed and ranked the calves based on their rate of growth. The logic being that faster growing was more productive.

The program required six inputs for each calf, dam (mother), sire (father), its weight and date when born, and the weight and date it was last weighed. The program then ranked the entire herd, and also ranked the herd against other herds using the same program. To give some indication of its impact, between the first and second year the performance of the herd improved by over 30%.

Back in the yards, getting accurate data for the program was part of what changed the nature of the cattle work. For example, the spring work now had pregnancy testing of the cows, as well as marking (removing testicles) from most of the male calves. The pregnancy testing is done by the vet, and the vet was paid by the hour, so it was important to ensure he had a ready supply of cows in the crush.

The crush is the cattle equivalent of the doctor's office – designed for a powerful and uncooperative bovine patient. Behind the crush is a race, which is where the next three patients queue, and behind that a funnel shaped yard that can hold around a dozen cows before they are herded into the race. Either side of these are larger holding yards, with the one off to the right split into front and back yards. Immediately in front of the crush are two side gates, and in front of the gates was the loading ramp (used to put cattle on and off trucks). The side gates can be arranged to direct the cattle left or right once they leave the crush. At the front of the crush are two strong vertical bars that can be quickly lowered into place either side of the cow's neck. At the back of the crush is a sliding gate that can prevent the cow going backwards.

After the cows and calves have been separated, the cows are usually in the larger yard on the left of the crush, and the calves are in the rear yard on the right of the race, which is the other side of the funnel shaped yard behind the race. The crew is generally arranged by family members with friends being an extra set of arms and legs. Debbie and I generally had the job of keeping the crush full, and applying the de-lice medicine to the backs of the cattle in the race. Barb and Cindy provided support to the work being done in the crush. Despite being left-handed, Cindy had the best handwriting, so she generally got the job of keeping records. This meant that Barb acted like a surgeon's assistant, handing dad the various tools he needed. This commonly included drenching (oral worm medicine), vaccination (injection), and shears (to trim ear hair so that ear tags can be easily read, and tails to prevent manure accumulating on the tail). Occasionally it includes horn cutters, and toe cutting – but these were rare on our farm as we bred Poll Herefords (Poll meaning hornless). It is usually an efficient production line, that steps up a gear when the vet is there.

The vet's job is pregnancy testing, which is done by inserting his arm into the anus of the cow and assessing the size of the womb. This occurred when the cow was in the crush at the same time that Dad was implementing all the other treatments. The pressure was on Dad to finish his tasks at around the same time as the vet. It was a bit like a pit stop in motor sport. The vet called out the number of weeks of pregnancy, Dad called out the tag number, and Cindy matched them up and wrote them down. The number of weeks is important as it determines which bull is the sire. This is because in late autumn we put one bull in with the heifers and each mob of cows, then five weeks later we rotate them. The rotation provides coverage for a non-performing or infertile bull. The pregnancy test becomes part of their performance assessment – if they come up with low pregnancy rates they are sold, no matter how good they looked.

The vet's presence at the back of the crush makes it much harder to get the cows up the race. Particularly as he was nearly as big as my dad and wore medical bright blue overalls. On one occasion when I was still shorter than the cows, he noticed that there was a delay and walked down the race to the funnel yard to help. This resulted in the cows trying hard to avoid him and pushing back against me so that I was pressed up against the fence. It took me a few minutes after they had cleared the cows away to get my breath back.

The yards were galvanised steel posts and mesh about two metres high, built on a large concrete slab next to a mullock heap, with a fence retaining yard between the yards and the adjacent paddock. The concrete sloped towards the back left, and unless it was summer, the concrete in all but the front right yard was covered in a brown soup like slop of accumulated cow manure, urine, and water. Gumboots were a must have item for those of us working in the back pens. Sometimes when we were bored, we would scoop some of the muck into the end of the plastic pipes we were using to move the cows and fling it at a target – usually a fence post, sometimes each other.

Once we had put all of either the calves or cows through the crush, we would break for lunch before going back to do whichever ones we had not done. Then the mob, minus any rejects, would be taken back to a paddock in the same method they had been brought into the yards, although generally more passively. The exception to this was at weaning. At weaning the calves, around nine months old, would be taken first into four separate paddocks. The bulls kept for breeding/sale would be taken to the bull paddock to be with the older bulls. The heifers kept for breeding would be taken to another paddock, while the heifers and steers to be sold into two other paddocks. Finally, the cows would be taken to their own paddock. This was always a difficult ride as the cows were keen to re-join their calves and with the calves in several different paddocks, they would try and go in different directions. It was one of the more exhilarating rides.

While the cows and calves were the more regular visitors to the yards, the bulls also had their turn. When not in with the cows, they were put in a paddock together. The first few days they were together generally involved a few fights as they sorted out their pecking order, hopefully without injury. Then, they would generally be fine. I recall one occasion when we had to get the bulls in because one of them, Woolo, had an eye infection. (All the bulls had names, and distinct personalities). I was older, late teens, at the time. We had herded them into the holding yards at the back, and we were trying to get Woolo into the funnel shaped yard, so that we could get him up the race and into the crush for the vet to look at his eye. He was the larger more dominant bull and some of the other bulls were taking advantage of his blind spot and the close confines to give him a shove. He was not happy. We seemed to be going in circles in our attempts to get him into the funnelled area. Suddenly, he turned and charged towards one of the other bulls that was moving alongside one of the fences. His head struck the other bull in the shoulder and the force of it pushed the two of them through the fence and out of the yards. We were always aware that the cattle were bigger and stronger than us, even so to be standing in the same pen when that happened was confronting. The force was so immense. The fence was thick welded metal, and they had gone through it like it was made from paper. I remember dad trying to force the bent panel back into shape, numerous belts with the sledgehammer hardly moved it at all, and Dad was hitting it hard.

Working cattle is largely bluff. Until the crush, the situation is in their favour, but because they choose to avoid the confrontation, they go from being one of 60 against four in an open field, to being isolated in a crush bereft of options.

In nature, an actual fight is avoided where possible. The bigger bull generally wins, and the bigger bull generally has a louder, deeper voice, so they bellow at each other to size each other up, avoiding the risk of injury from actually fighting. In lots of other cases, it often comes down to who has the strongest presence. Ideally the strong presence is also non-threatening – because a threatened animal will fight or flee, and most of the time you just want them to comply.

Dad had the ideal presence. His big presence radiated well beyond him, but it radiated calm. As kids working the cattle, we worked on adjusting our presence. We called it 'stock sense', knowing when to be big, when to be small. It is hard to explain, even harder to teach – some of our friends got it, others didn't. Those working the back yards needed to have a big presence, those helping at the crush a smaller presence. Part of the presence in the back of the cattle yards is convincing the cow that you are never going to stop until it does what you want. When we were little, that was really the only thing we had. Certainly, the whacks with the pipe were more noise than impact, and when you see the forces the cattle apply to each other, we were not forcing them to do anything, they were just trying to escape the annoyance, as we would try and avoid a fly or diving bird.

The other factor that helped us was that my parents also sold the aggressive cows, so that we generally had a placid herd. We also treated the cattle in a way that helped keep them to be placid, even the bulls were generally well behaved, particularly after we got a reputation for breeding bulls and started selling them. This was because unlike the steers, heifers and cows that were sent off to market to be sold, bull buyers came to the farm. It was a process not unlike buying a puppy from a dog breeder, only on a larger scale. Part of this process involved herding the bulls into the yards, separating out the young bulls from the older bulls. The young bulls were generally sold at around two years of age, and the older bulls were there as a breeding reference as if to say, This young bull was sired by that big bull, he will look like that some day'.

Because of the risk of interbreeding, we generally did not use our own bulls. Hawkeye was the exception. Even as a calf he stood out, at six months old he was as big as his mother. He grew into a large bull, and his calves always rated highly on the computer's herd calculation. Unlike Woolo, he was also generally easy to manage. However, as time went on it became harder to use him for breeding as his offspring kept being added to the breeding herd.

Cattle work was such a dominant part of my childhood, occupying at least a week of each school holidays, that it is easy to remember the overall process, but harder to remember specific incidents as they tend to blend into an overall theme. However, one of the key things to come out of the cattle work, and Dad riding Max, was that if Mum was not with us then one of the kids had to drive the Landcruiser. And from the age of nine, that defaulted to me, and I have numerous memories of driving related incidents.

Driving

My first memory of driving was sitting on Dad's lap and being given control of the steering wheel as we drove down the road. He instructed me to adjust where I was looking based on the speed of the Landcruiser. The faster we were going, the further ahead I should be looking. This was a lesson I learned well and applied when I was given full control of the vehicle around the farm at the age of nine. I was short, even for a nine-year-old, which meant that I looked through the steering wheel, not over it. The angle of my vision meant that I could not see the ground for at least 25 metres in front of the bonnet. So, applying the logic of my first driving lesson, I drove fast so that I could see where I was going.

Apparently, it was difficult to see me from outside the vehicle. On one occasion I terrified the vet. He had arrived at the cattle yards early, and when he saw the Landcruiser approaching at high speed without being able to see anyone in the driver's seat, he was convinced the vehicle was out of control.

In between my first lesson and frightening the vet was lots of time behind the wheel of the tractor at very low speeds. My oldest sister Debbie had paved the way in this regard. We both started with Dad handing over control of the tractor as part of feeding out the hay, with my turn coming shortly after hers. To give some sense of the level of skill required, prior to us doing it, no one was in control. Dad had just pointed the tractor in the right direction, set it in motion and got off the tractor and onto the trailer to feed out the hay. The problem with this method was that he had to keep an eye on where the tractor was going and get back on the tractor to redirect it if it strayed toward something substantial, like a tree or a dam. The cattle were smart enough to get out of the way, and more interested in the freshly delivered hay than to stand in front of the tractor anyway.

The reason I got my turn so early was that Deb had been instructed to drive toward a distant tree, and many minutes later she dutifully drove straight into it. With this experience fresh in his mind, Dad's instructions to me were to drive in a big circle avoiding trees, dams, steep hills, stumps, and other objects. There was no power steering, so when I wanted to turn, I would stand up on one side of the wheel and heave like it was a helm on a sailing ship.

Tractor controls are different to car controls, particularly back then. The tractor had a single seat between the two large back wheels with a steel mesh platform around it welded onto the axle between the two back wheels. Behind the seat was air and various functional parts of the tractor, including the tow bar to which the trailer was attached. The front and back wheels were uncovered, except there was a vertical panel from the mesh up to the top of the rear wheels. In front of the seat, between an adult driver's legs, was the gearbox, and in front of that the steering wheel. This tractor did not have a foot throttle, rather a hand throttle that stayed where you put it. The clutch was on the left side of the engine, and the brake (which could be split left and right) was on the right of the engine. In front of the steering wheel was the fuel tank, and in front of the fuel tank was the engine. Either side of the engine were the two front wheels.

Sitting in the driver's seat I could not see where I was going, so I would drive by moving between the platforms on either side of the raised gearbox and gearstick. I was too small and light to use either the clutch or the brakes, and I was told not to touch the throttle. If this all sounds dangerous, it should be remembered that Dad was unable to run after his injury, and we were going slow enough that after stepping off the trailer, he could walk faster than the tractor, get on and take over the controls from me. It also explains why no one got hurt when Debbie drove into the tree.

The Landcruiser also had a hand throttle, and some extra low gear settings. This was how I transitioned from steering the tractor to steering the Landcruiser, and then discovered that if I pushed up against the steering wheel I could push down against the clutch and the brakes and actually stop the vehicle. I was now on my way to driving. The Landcruiser was a 1965 model. After a decade spent dripping in mud, it was battered and rusty, but still very sturdy. The major flaw in its design as a farm vehicle was it had drum brakes, which did not work when they had water in them – which on our farm in winter was most of the time. Driving fast with faulty brakes has its challenges, particularly when reaching the pedals is also a stretch.

One of the things my parents spent money on when they purchased Murray's farm was the farm tracks. With a huge supply of mine tailings on hand, we did not need to purchase any gravel. Murray had already put gravel tracks in place on the main tracks of what was once his farm, from the side road through the cattle yards to the log cabin. The new works now connected our house to these tracks and extended it through to the hayshed near the cattle yards. We also now had a front driveway finishing in a circle in front of the house. The only problem with the front drive was that it went through a paddock and so required opening two gates, while the original drive (now back drive as it arrived at the back of the house) had no gates. So, in true country tradition, the front drive was as rarely used as the front door.

I recall the distinct sucking sound that tractor tyres make on wet ground when the thick chunky tread is withdrawn from the moulded earth. It was a common sound on our farm in winter, particularly before the gravelled tracks were made. The gravelled farm tracks followed the old tracks, which in winter had been a boggy mess almost axle deep in places. The gravel kept the tyres on the surface but did not prevent the water pooling on the tracks. As kids we took delight in the Landcruiser going through the puddles at speed to get the water to spray up. Smaller puddles and lower speeds just sprayed sideways, but larger puddles and high speeds also created a vertical spray onto the bonnet and the windscreen. A combination of a large puddle and high speed could even get the spray over the roof and onto the tray. Now that I had control of the vehicle, this became something to aim for.

The track from the house had a gate at the hayshed, then went through a large paddock (referred to as the '100 Acres'), before another gate to another paddock ('40 Acres'), then a further gate where it joined what had been Murray's farm ('Cattle Yard paddock'). The path through the 100 Acres started at the top of a rise, then about half-way were two hills in quick succession, after which was a flat section, then a sharp left turn, followed by a sharp right turn, then the gate. In winter there was usually a small puddle between the two hills, and a larger deeper puddle just before the sharp left turn. To get the spray over the roof the vehicle had to be going at its top speed of 40 miles per hour (65 km/h) as it hit the larger deeper puddle. To achieve that, you needed to be in top gear (3rd) and accelerate at the bottom of the first rise, go over the two hills like a rollercoaster, hit the water, then turn blindly (as the spray prevented any vision), and start pumping the brakes to get the water out of them in time to stop before the gate. It is a sequence that I remember well as I attempted it so often it became muscle memory. Which is not to say that I always succeeded.

On one of my earliest attempts, I failed to get enough water out of the brakes before the gate, and subsequently rolled into it. Barb was with me, so we got out to inspect the damage. We were relieved to find both the gate and vehicle intact. The gate was made of galvanised iron frame with heavy duty wire cross-hatching. There was too much pressure on the chain for the gate to be opened, so I got back into the driver's seat and reversed the vehicle. Which was when it became apparent that part of the gate and the protruding bumper bar had become entangled. As a result, the gate was bent out of shape and the chain stretched to breaking point. Having learnt little from our mistakes, Barb and I decided that driving forward was now the solution and distorted the gate further. At this point we inspected the entanglement more closely and then decided that it was beyond the physical capability of two kids aged seven and nine to fix and walked home to get help.

Dad calmly listened to our description of events, drove the family car down for a closer inspection and decided that some bigger tools were required. Shortly after this we were back on site with sledgehammer, crowbar, and a five-tonne roller (towed behind the tractor to flatten roads). Dad had a plan. He used the crowbar and the sledgehammer to manoeuvre various bits of the gate off the bumper while I edged the vehicle back and forth as instructed. Once the vehicle was free, he undid the hinges so that we could also undo the chain. Then came the finale. The badly bent gate was taken to a flat part of the road, then the roller was driven over it. The intent was to flatten it. What actually happened was that the gate wrapped around the roller in a semi-circle. It then sprang off dramatically once released from the weight of the roller.

The now semi-circular gate was eventually beaten back into the right shape and refitted to the gate posts. That I did not get in 'trouble' for hitting the gate in the first place was not really a surprise. Dad always had the view that mistakes made while learning were part of life and was very forgiving of them. What irritated him was people not being prepared to give things a go.

Dad's attitude was matched by my grade four teacher. His name was Mr Lipton, and he was an inspirational educator. While I have forgotten whole school years, I still remember different activities from grade four. My memories of Haddon Primary School were all outdoors. My strongest memory of grade two, my first year at Ballarat Grammar, was learning our maths times-tables around a record player as we progressively lost our baby teeth. I also remember the junior school headmaster trying to drag a boy from the room after he had stood on a table and showed his penis to the entire class. The boy had returned his penis inside his pants, but he grabbed at a table shared by four kids on the way out and dragged it until it blocked the door of the classroom. Grade three I only recall the school trip. But by grade four, I remember learning things and actually wanting to learn more.

The big difference was that Mr Lipton wanted us to think and encouraged us to try new things. He would introduce us to new concepts and invite us to invent solutions. One of these was building a rocket that would fly across the classroom. He showed us pictures from a book that had a rocket made from a cigar case, suspended from a wire, that was propelled across the room by burning match heads. It looked simple enough. So, we were asked to bring the various components to school so that we could try it ourselves.

This was not the first time we had arrived home to ask our parents for a strange collection of items to take to school for Mr Lipton. Our parents seemed to lack any concern or curiosity about why we needed to take matches, wire, and cigar cases to school. Perhaps if they had been more interested, we might have ended up with more appropriate equipment for the task at hand. Instead of piano wire or fishing wire which could have been held taut and relatively frictionless, I provided fencing wire, which even when unrolled had bends and kinks in it. Meanwhile another child provided cigar cases that turned out to be plastic. So, the class's first attempt at a rocket blast across the room was a spectacular failure. The match heads caught fire readily enough, but instead of propelling the cigar case they set it on fire, at which point melted bits of burning plastic started to drop onto the tables and chairs below, then the main body of match heads caught fire creating a mini explosion that sprayed burning plastic throughout the room. Fortunately, nobody was hurt, although most of the chairs and tables had permanent scorch marks.

Many a teacher would abandon the activity at this point. Not Mr Lipton, he asked us to think about what had gone wrong and to come up with a plan to make it work better the next time. We had at least a dozen attempts at getting the rocket to work over the next few weeks before it finally did. Each attempt improving on the last and only one of them surpassing the initial attempt for danger. That was because of Michael, and the danger was introduced by him intentionally.

Michael was one of four Michaels in my class and as we were at school in the '70s none of them were called by their first name. Michael's surname was Croatian and most of the teachers had trouble pronouncing it, but within weeks of teaching him they were well practiced at yelling it. Michael was smart and permanently bored at school and so entertained himself by creating mayhem. In grade four he became my best friend at school because Tony was in grade five and now had different times for recess and lunch.

My friendship with Michael had its origins in games of piggy-back fights. These involved kids pairing up, one rider, one horse, and then crowding together trying to dismount the other riders. Michael was the tallest in the class and I was the smallest. Where other pairs took turns at being horse or rider, I was always the rider. As a combination we became unbeatable. Part of this was because while most other horses simply carried their riders and tried to stay upright, Michael was trained in martial arts and used all his limbs. This made being his rider more challenging as I often had one or none of his arms to help me stay on. But having successfully ridden a bucking Trigger at home, I was up for the challenge. None of our opponents were up for the chaos that Michael unleashed with his free limbs. Sometimes he helped me tackle the opposing riders, but most of the time he attacked the other horses, taking advantage of their arms being preoccupied by holding up their riders. He generally preferred to trick them into dropping their rider by tickling them, pinching their nose, or even putting his hand in their pockets. This would cause them to flinch or squirm and subsequently drop their rider. If the opposing horse could withstand this trickery, then he resorted to martial arts moves, tripping them over, or bending their thumbs or arms into unwanted positions. After a while the others would gang up on us. When we still won, they stopped playing.

Back in the classroom, Michael managed to hide a firework rocket inside one of the cigar-case rockets. It was notable for the fact that it was the first one to move along the wire, but then it got caught on one of the kinks in the wire, melted the metal cigar case and dropped onto the floor and then shot across the floor before hitting the wall and burning out. Without waiting for an enquiry, Mr Lipton immediately sent Michael to the headmaster for punishment. Michael was often assumed to be guilty of whatever mischief was happening and most of the time they were right, even if lacking justice. For his part Michael simply took the punishment, which was either being caned (struck with a wooden cane) or being struck with the sandshoe – which was a running shoe that had all but the sole and heal removed. The school generally preferred the later as it did not leave marks on the recipient.

Grade four was also my first experience of Michael's home life. I had stayed at Wayne's once or twice before he left the school, and at Tony's so often it was like a second home. Wayne's reminded me of our old house, and Tony's of my cousin's. Tony lived in a large house and had a nurturing mum and a scary but largely absent dad, as well as siblings, dogs, and horses. Michael's home life was different.

Michael lived in an older house walking distance from the school. Technically, he lived in half the house as it had been divided down the middle, with his grandmother living on one side and Michael and his parents living on the other side. Both Michael's parents worked at the caravan factory and the plaster internal walls of the house had been covered over or replaced by the fake-wood panelling that was fashionable in caravans in the 1970s. Both of his parents were immigrants, his mother was Dutch and his father Croatian. I think they both were university educated, although this was not recognised in their current jobs. They were both tall and athletic, and Michael would always be tall for his age and intellectually and athletically gifted. He had no siblings, but he did have a very devoted dog. Tarzan was a large and very well-fed Labrador. Like his owner, Tarzan seemed impervious to physical challenges and discomfort. These were qualities that would also be required of the guests at Michael's grade four birthday sleepover.

The sleepover itself was in a caravan in Michael's backyard. It was a large relatively new one at the time, and remains the only caravan I have ever slept in. Although, I did not sleep much. The first hours of the party had been spent in typical fashion for a kid's birthday party in the '70s. We were overloaded on food with no nutritional value and large amounts of sugar and preservatives and had played very physical games with an excessive amount of energy. We had played pass-the-parcel, with only one prize in it, and had ice cream cake in the shape of an elephant. Then, as the sugar left our systems, we had to sort a place to put our sleeping bags so we could talk ourselves to sleep. It was at this point that Michael decided to deviate from the standard party script. He decided we were going to stay up all night. Given that most of us were accustomed to getting up early and only saw midnight on New Year's Eve, staying up all night seemed like an impossible task.

What we did not count on was that Michael was on a mission. If he spotted one of us going to sleep, he would do something to wake us up. Early on some water in the face or a loud noise would do the trick, but as the night wore on more extreme measures were required to keep our young, exhausted minds awake. At some point Michael went from popping balloons, to stretching out the broken balloon pieces and then snapping them on our skin. It was startlingly painful. And so, we all managed to greet the dawn. I have never been more relieved to see the sunrise, or more let down by the sense of occasion.

But the strangeness of the occasion didn't end there. After managing a small amount of sleep, we were woken by Michael's mother for breakfast. The breakfast itself was not unusual. But shortly after breakfast, with stomachs still full and sleep still lacking, Michael's father agreed to Michael's request to play an unpronounceable game with us. I have no idea if it existed outside their family, but the stated aim of the game was that we were to try and get to the other end of the narrow hallway, in our path was Michael's father, and apparently there were no other rules.

We had numerous attempts, but none of us ever made it to the other end of the hall. If we rushed him as a pack, he found ways to make us get in each-other's way. If we went at him individually, he simply picked us off. The end result was always the dozen of us piled up in a stack with him controlling the top of the pile. He must have been strong, because despite the inherent violence and mayhem in the game, he never hurt any of us. Even when we managed to trip him over, he made sure he did not land on any of us.

It was shortly after that game ended that our parents arrived to take us home. My mum was one of the first to arrive, but one of the last to leave. Michael's mum was keen to get to know her as she had heard lots about me from Michael. I think she hoped that I would be a good influence on him. Mum had also heard a lot about Michael, some from me, some from my sisters, and a lot from the school. The school had advised Mum not to encourage the friendship. Which is probably the reason that despite Michael and I being close friends through to the end of school and beyond, in all that time he never came to our farm.

Michael's party was not the only memorable birthday party that year. Back then, everyone had their birthday party at home, and most only every second year. One of these was Nick's, he lived near Skipton almost an hour from Ballarat, and so the parents of the kids invited had decided to car-pool. My Mum did the drop-off in our station wagon, with two bench seats and the back of the car all in use. The pick-up was done by Scott's mum in a Jaguar.

The party was memorable for two reasons. The first was the collapse of the two-storey tree house. Like all tree houses that I knew, it had been constructed by the kids out of spare bits of timber and materials that they had managed to cobble together over numerous holidays. We had a similar one at home in a large old pine tree near the house that we had made while the new house was being built. It needed a ladder to get to and then wrapped its way around the tree trunk and various branches over three different levels. We enjoyed building it and extending it more than just hanging out in it. While it had timber floors, most of the walls were made from wool bale canvas. From the ground it looked like a bloated sailing ship had crashed into the tree. Nick's tree house was made from timber and Masonite sheets, it had two levels, and the bottom one was on the ground. At one point during the party, we were all in the top level, which caused one of the supporting walls to give way, so that we all tumbled into the bottom level and out of the cubby. We all thought it was great fun, although Nick was a little sad at the damage to his tree house until his older brother reassured him that it would be easy to rebuild.

The other reason it was memorable was the trip home. Scott's mum had brought his twin three-year-old brothers with her and was possibly surprised at the number of kids she was taking back. Certainly, it was a very full car. I shared the front passenger seat, designed for one adult, with two other boys. The back seat was a mass of bodies and noise. On leaving Nick's farm we had to cross a railway line, and Scott's mum was worried about damaging the bottom of the car and went over it slowly. What most of us in the car did not know was that the new kid Paul had opened one of the rear passenger doors apparently to try and hear if a train was coming. We only found out about this when we were 10 minutes down the road and it was discovered that one of Scott's younger twins was missing. It was a very fast drive back to the railway crossing, where we were fortunate to find the twin unharmed. Paul was an odd kid, but what none of us could understand was how he could just shut the door and allow the car to drive off after having allowed a small child to fall onto the road.

I remember telling Mum all about the collapsed tree house and the drive home. She looked pale and scared. I thought it was one of the twins being left at a railway crossing, or the very fast driving. Whatever it was, the next weekend we had to dismantle our tree house. Dad helped us, so it was done quickly. It also showed up the poor quality of the construction.

One of the big differences I noticed between Haddon Primary School and Ballarat Grammar other than the number of kids, was the number of different places we went. In grade four alone we went on least six different trips. We were studying bushrangers at school, and I remember going to the Old Melbourne Gaol – and then afterwards we also went to a Chinese restaurant and had a banquet before we got back on the bus and headed home. It was not unusual for the school to try and combine multiple experiences into a trip, even if they were academically unconnected. When we went to Swan Hill, we explored an old-time settlement there as well as paddle steamers. But not to miss out on an educational opportunity, we had stopped in on a tour of a pheasant farm. The tour started with a show-and-tell of the different types of pheasants and how pretty they were, and then moved onto watching the birds get processed, starting with the beheading of live birds. In the 1970s there was no consciousness of people being triggered, and any kid who had trouble dealing with some industrial butchering was mocked by their classmates. Certainly, those of us who lived on farms wondered what all the fuss was about.

The most memorable trip was to Sovereign Hill, the now famous gold mining theme park, set in the 1850s. It was relatively new at the time, and much less sophisticated. There was even debate amongst the kids at school as to whether it or another local theme park 'Kryal Castle' built in the style of a medieval castle was better. The favoured feature of the castle was that it sold miniature cross bows that could accurately shoot matchsticks across a room. It was just one of many dangerous attractions that were key selling points of most of the theme parks at the time. Most of them had 'enter at own risk' type signs and expected patrons to keep themselves out of harm's way. The most extreme example of this was the Lion Park about halfway between Ballarat and Melbourne. It was very popular when it opened, and while the school did not go there, we did visit it as a family. The main attraction was that you could drive your own car through the lion enclosure. On entering, patrons were simply asked to ensure they wound up their windows and told not to get out of their cars even if they had a mechanical failure. As far as I am aware everyone did and there were no issues. Risks were accepted as part of life, and people got accustomed to recognising them and dealing with them. Back at the Sovereign Hill trip, we were not doing anything quite as dangerous – but we were going to be there when it was not open to the public. This was because we were going to be making our own bushranger film.

It was an amalgamation of various bushranger stories and Mr Lipton's imagination. It also taught us a bit about the trickery of film making. The outsides of the buildings we ran into, did not match the buildings we then appeared inside of. We ran into and out of the same mine tunnel but on the film, it looked like we ran in one place and out another. We filmed scenes out of sequence, at Sovereign Hill in the morning, and at an abandoned farmhouse in the afternoon. But these were spliced together so that we looked like we went from town to farm and back again. It was a silent movie, so we also had the old fashion dialogue and description cards. It was typical of Mr Lipton in that we learnt a lot and had fun doing it.

Another trip we went on with Mr Lipton included at least two classes and had us staying in cabins, I think it may have been a location owned by the scouts. I only remember two things about it. One was that a boy, possibly as a dare, put a considerable amount of toothpaste on his penis which caused him significant pain. I was not there when he applied it, but it is hard to forget seeing him screaming and pant-less with his penis clasped in one hand as he rushed toward the toilet block. Perhaps Mr Lipton and the other teachers were trying to erase that memory when they embarked on an ill-fated tour of the cabins that evening. They had covered their hands and forearms in flour from the kitchen and moved around outside the cabins making scary noises. Inside our cabin we were making so much noise we did not really hear them until some of the kids in another cabin started screaming and we stopped talking so we could listen to what was going on outside. It was during one of these quiet intervals as we stared out into the gloom that Mr Lipton moved his ghost like hand across our cabin window giving us a fright and causing us to jump back from the open louvre window. The ghost hand was then thrust through the window and accompanied by a guttural growl. It did not have the intended effect as Scott (the brother of the twins) leapt forward and slammed the lever down on the louvre windows jamming the windowpanes across the intruding forearm and causing its owner to scream out in pain. We then heard Mr Lipton's familiar voice asking us to release the window.

I believe I had a particularly good education, although my school report cards would suggest that it may have been wasted on me. The most commonly used word was potential, and the most common theme was some puzzlement that the understanding I displayed in the classroom was so rarely reflected in the test results. What was never questioned, and possibly still isn't, was whether the tests measured understanding or the ability to regurgitate names, facts, and dates. I also learnt a lot from my school experiences that was not formally part of the curriculum. One of these was taking the bus to school – which began at the start of grade five.

School Bus

The school bus was an education like no other. We first started taking the bus when Debbie was in year eight, Cindy was in grade six, I was in grade five and Barb just grade three. The bus was introduced to replace the train, and we caught it from the very first day it was available. The train had run from Skipton into Ballarat, and it was what enabled lots of country kids to get a high school education. For the kids at the end of the line it was an hour trip each way, which makes for long school days. We never caught the train largely due to its reputation for poor behaviour and unreliable arrivals. The kids said they behaved badly because they stopped in random places along the track, the train operator said that it had to stop in random places because the kids behaved badly. Regardless of who was at fault, the numbers dwindled on the train until it seemed feasible to replace it with a bus.

The bus stop in Haddon was at the level crossing nearest to where the train siding had been. I recall on the first day that Debbie was happy chatting to some of her friends from primary school who were now going to high school. Meanwhile the other three of us young ones looked on in awe and trepidation. The bus arrived late and full. Apparently, there were lots more families willing to put their kids on the bus, compared to the old train. The bus driver yelled at the kids on the bus to move back and we were squeezed onto the bus with just enough space for the door to close behind us. Over the coming days and weeks, the bus route was divided up until that one bus load was spread across four buses, all still with more kids than seats.

The organisation of the country school buses into Ballarat was quite impressive. The various district buses all came into a central point, exchanged passengers, and then went to designated schools. The process was reversed in the afternoon. The local newspaper quoted it as being 2,000 kids changing buses in five minutes twice a day, so there must have been about 40 buses involved. When we first started on the buses the exchange was in the main street opposite Saint Patrick's College – but after some complaints from the residents it was moved to be next to the lake. Once you got into the swing of it, it was relatively easy, get off the bus you came in on, find the bus you need to go out on. The difference in atmosphere on the buses varied with the kids – each becoming a mini culture complete with pecking order.

The district bus I caught started in Smythesdale and went through Haddon, most of the kids went to one of the two tech schools. The second bus I caught went to Ballarat Grammar, although on some days it also took the overflow of kids who went to one of the tech schools. The district bus had its fair share of rough and tumble, but all the kids knew that their parents knew each other so it also had some unspoken boundaries – most of the time. The buses themselves were generally of poor quality, resulting in multiple occasions when two bus routes would be squeezed into one, and the bus drivers themselves had unique characteristics.

I caught the bus for eight years and watched different age groups of kids establish their claims on various seats, build and destroy friendships, and various other things all the while being entertained. The highest status seat on the bus was the backseat, and particularly the middle of it. I never sat there. 'M' was younger than me and got on at my stop, and for the last two years of my school bus trips – the middle of the back seat was hers. This was possibly the only position of status she had in life. She did not wear it elegantly, but she certainly held it proudly. On one occasion a boy her age that was part of the backseat gang was dared into sitting in the middle seat ahead of 'M' getting on the bus. Feeling that his moment of glory had come he accepted the challenge.

'M' got on the bus, yelled at the boy to get out of her seat in very strong language, and when he grinned and said no, she strode down the aisle and promptly punched his nose so hard she broke it. Pushing him aside she took up her throne and put her feet up on the back of the arm rests of the seats on either side with a look of triumph on her face. Nobody on the bus, that day or each and every other day she did it, ever had the courage to tell 'M' that the combination of her foot position and short skirt provided the entire bus with a view of her underwear.

This was not the only blood spilt on the bus. On another occasion a boy was reluctantly convinced by his brother to get his ear pierced. It was not having a pierced ear that was the issue, it was the method he was not keen on. The ear stud had been donated by one of the girls on the bus that this boy was keen on, and he did not want to appear ungrateful. And when she said that she had her ears pierced and it had not hurt, he also did not want to appear chicken. Particularly now that most of the bus was watching on.

The reason for his reluctance was, I thought, quite reasonable. The equipment being proposed for the task had been extracted from a school pencil case. It was a standard issue compass and eraser. The eraser was to be held behind the earlobe to prevent the compass going into his neck after it had pierced a hole in the earlobe. It was a bad plan. Eventually everything was in place, different kids volunteered to hold different parts of his head and the apparatus, and the tip of the compass was lined up with his earlobe, with the stud on standby ready to be inserted into the newly made hole. We all gasped as the compass was pulled back, and groaned as the bus bounced and the compass was thrust into another part of the ear (not the earhole) causing blood to spurt on all those gathered to assist the proceeding. His ear recovered unscarred, but he never did get his ear pierced.

Some of boys were into cars and motor bikes and would often trade vehicle parts with each other while on the school bus. On this occasion one of them got onto the bus after school with a particularly heavy school bag. He was halfway down the aisle when the bottom of the bag gave way and the contents spilled onto the floor of the bus. It was right next to where I was sitting. I was not surprised to find that there were no schoolbooks. I was expecting some sort of car parts, but there was just a single item. A large high-quality bench vice, with the words 'St Pats W-Work #3' engraved on it. I am not sure what else he got from his time at the school, but he probably got more from the school than they were trying to teach him.

It was not just car parts that were exchanged on the school bus. Occasionally so were pets. On one occasion a ferret got out on the bus. It happened to be on one of the old buses that had no bag racks, so the floor was strewn with bags, which the fashion of the day dictated were not zipped up – so the ferret darted in and out of school bags as it tried to get away from the increasing din of children screaming and yelling.

Another time on one of the old buses, we had a fill-in driver who had an issue with bags in the aisle. Given the bus had no bag racks and the floor was flat and slippery, bags in the aisle was inevitable. It sent this driver nuts, at one of the stops he got out of his seat and started picking up bags and throwing them out of the open bus door. It happened to be our stop, and I remember being startled as the bus door opened and bags were flung over our heads as we moved to get onto the bus. He kept shouting at us, 'I told them, I told them!'. Meanwhile inside the bus kids were yelling at him and trying to get past him and us to retrieve their bags before he drove off again. He was not alone in being strange. Another driver stopped the bus on the way home and refused to continue driving until we all apologised to him for what we had done. While we were all willing to parrot back any apology to get home, he had made the task impossible by not giving us any clues as to what we had done wrong. His grasp of English was not much better than his grasp on reality and so we spent a few minutes exchanging puzzled looks before he called us all cretins and continued our journey home.

All of these instances were spread across many years and in between were 100s of uneventful bus trips. Although at the start of grade five, being part of this cocktail of high school behaviour was mesmerising, particularly when it became apparent that most of the bus drivers happily turned a blind eye to behaviour on the bus, providing it did not damage the bus, or prevent it from reaching its destination. In the first two years, smoking was so prevalent that the bus was chock full of it, and we all got off smelling of cigarette smoke.

What also became apparent in those early years was the power good looking girls had over even the largest and roughest of the boys. Fortunately for me, something about me caused some sort of mothering instinct to kick in with these girls so that I was off limits to the often violent 'pranks' played by the bigger kids on those less able to defend themselves. It was also fortunate that in the summer leading into grade five, I finally kicked the habit of sucking my thumb.

Embarrassing Milestones

There are milestones in life that everyone goes through, often with a sense of pride. Grade five included two milestones for me that were so overdue they were more an embarrassment than an achievement. The first of these was not sucking my thumb.

My parents had tried many things over many years to get Cindy and I to stop sucking our thumbs. They succeeded with Cindy well before me, and had resorted to big promises to try and get me to finally end what was an unhealthy habit – particularly on a farm. It was something I did unconsciously, often being surprised when asked to 'stop sucking your thumb' or 'get your thumb out of your mouth'. I was also appropriately disgusted on occasions when I compared my two thumbs and found the sucked one clean, and the other filthy. It was not a habit I was proud of, but it was a habit I had a hard time shaking.

It would be Tony's mum that would help me kick it. Apparently, she sucked her thumb as a child and so had some sympathy for my plight. Even without that connection she was such a kind and supportive person I always felt that she was there for me. I was staying at the beach with them for two weeks, and the deal was quite simple – every day I didn't suck my thumb I got 20 cents. This was enough to buy a 'flake' chocolate bar and a small can of drink. Given I never got any pocket money this was an amazing deal. I think in the two weeks I missed out just twice, on days three and six. It also helped that there was always something to do.

Tony was the youngest of four children, all adopted, none genetically related. He had two older sisters and an older brother, all four of them were very different personalities, all of them were encouraged to be themselves and to respect others. It was a household in which I felt completely at home, whether it was at their beach house, or at their small farm on the outskirts of Ballarat. It was not uncommon for Tony and I to spend the majority of our holidays together, some at my house, some at his. And just as at my house his visits generally coincided with my sisters also having friends to stay, when I stayed with Tony, his siblings also had friends to stay.

The year I stopped sucking my thumb was the second of six successive years in which I would spend the first two weeks of January at their beach house, and every year his sisters would also invite the same friends. Tony's older brother Peter often did not have a friend to stay, preferring his own company most of the time. The sisters' friends were also sisters, and one of the things the four of them had in common was a liking for horse riding. Every evening we would go to where the horses were staying (across the road from the golf course) and then follow them with the family dogs (three of them) to the stretch of beach between Point Lonsdale and Ocean Grove. They would ride off toward the sunset, while we would throw the ball and various bits of driftwood for the dogs.

In the first two years, during the day we would generally be left to do as we pleased so long as we were around for mealtimes. We roamed freely along the front and back beach, out along the pier as well as under it, explored around the light house and into Buckley's cave. At night-time we would chat and play cards, and occasionally watch movies on the TV – or listen to them hiding behind the couch whilst patting one of the dogs. In the process we all got to know one another well.

What I did very little of was swim. There were two main reasons for this that reinforced each other, the first was that I could not swim, and the second was that I hated cold water. I say they are related because it takes time to learn to swim and I got cold so quickly that I did not learn to do anything but shiver.

Which brings me to the other embarrassing milestone. Toward the end of grade five, I received my certificate for swimming 15 metres. Fortunately, my friend Nick also received the award at the same time as me, because every other child called up to the front of the assembly that day was at least two years younger than us. What made this even less of a proud moment for me was the knowledge that I had cheated on the test, touching the ground a couple of times on my way across the pool.

My lack of swimming ability was one of the differences between my father and me. Dad was big and had swum in state swimming carnivals, I was small and sank like a stone. He loved the water – I was terrified of it. In my experience it was usually cold, opaque and full of dangerous animals. This was a view reinforced by seeing the movie *Jaws* while staying at the beach with Tony's family. That night several of us found ourselves in Tony's mum's bedroom in search of safety from the shark.

But sharks were a new fear. Preceding them were leeches and yabbies – both of which I had seen firsthand. We did not have a pool at home. Instead, we swam in the dams and waterhole. I recall preparing to swim in a recently created dam in one of the paddocks. Debbie had got ready before the rest of us and had launched in to be the first to swim from one end to the other. She arrived at the other end covered in leeches. We never swam in that dam again.

The dam nearest the house was a great source of yabbies (small freshwater crayfish). Putting a chunk of meat in on a string would retrieve one or two yabbies, and yabbies saw young feet in the same way. The waterhole had a spring in the bottom of it and was over 12 metres deep. While the water was clear, it was surrounded by the steep walls of open cut mining and was permanently cold. Even when we pumped the water from this through irrigation channels 100s of metres long, the water was still like ice.

The only dam I was prepared to swim in was the one near the hayshed, about 100 metres from the house. At the start of summer, it would be full and around 50 metres across. By the end of summer, it would be less than 15 metres across. Most of the change happened just before Christmas when the water level would retreat from a large shallow expanse never more than a few feet deep into the part of the dam that had been dug out to build the dam bank. I enjoyed the shallows, floating on blow-up matts and watching the dragonflies and listening to the frogs. The main dam was not as good, as the bottom was 20 cm of soft mud, the water was completely opaque, and below the first 30 cm it was cold. The water also dyed all our bathers a murky brown, something very unwelcome to my sisters and their friends when their bathers included white fabric. The main appeal of this dam was that it did not have leeches or yabbies.

The reason for this was an accident in winter a few years earlier when we had been throwing large clumps of dirt into the dam to try and make a big splash. One of the Cobb boys picked up the salt-block and hurled it in before we could stop him. Salt-blocks are an expensive combination of minerals in a large block that cows lick of their own accord to improve their own mineral balance. Apparently, they also keep away leeches and yabbies if thrown into a dam. I am not sure how we came to realise that this dam was without these unwanted swimming companions, but this soon became the place we sought on summer days. In the summer after the house was extended, we dragged part of the old picket fence down to the dam and strapped it on to some old 44-gallon drums to make a jetty and diving board.

The following summer I received an inflatable dinghy for Christmas, as well as a pair of floaties. The dinghy also had oars. I think it was hoped that having me spend time on the water would reduce my fear of it. That Christmas Aunt Sal also came to stay. In the following years her presence would be as much a part of Christmas as presents and overeating. On this summer day Sal occupied most of the dinghy and her legs extended beyond it. I sat on top of her and tried to row us across the dam. We had a lot of laughs, but we did not make much progress. Then Debbie thought it would be fun to tip us out of the dinghy.

She succeeded and with a great splash we were plunged into the water and the dinghy was flipped upside down. The floaties did their job and brought me back to the surface, but it was inside the upturned dinghy. On the outside of the dinghy, Sal had resurfaced, but the laughter had been replaced by panic as they searched for me, knowing I could not swim. Shortly afterwards they heard my voice muffled by the dinghy and fun was restored to the dam.

At the end of grade five I had a far more stressful ride in an inflatable dinghy. I was visiting Michael, who had received an inflatable dinghy for Christmas. He lived near Lake Wendouree and had been on the lake several times already. He let his parents know that I had my swimming certificate and that we would not venture far from shore (the lake itself is two km across). We made the short journey to the lake, he carried the dinghy, and I carried the oars, while his dog Tarzan followed along. Things started off normally enough, as we kept reasonably close to shore and Tarzan was more interested in the ducks and swans than in us. But then Michael started getting bored.

He decided we could go a little further out, and in response to some people on the shore he called Tarzan away from the swans and ducks. The labrador had no trouble swimming after us and was soon attempting to get on board. Michael told me he was worried about Tarzan damaging the dinghy and so Tarzan was lifted in and dumped on top of me. Then the dinghy started to deflate. We were at least 100 metres from shore, and I had no floaties. I became genuinely frightened. Michael watched me intently, like a curious scientist, then started rowing to shore. But the weight of the three of us seemed to prevent us getting anywhere. Michael then decided to see if he could touch the bottom with one of the oars, and having succeeded promptly jumped overboard with the water up around his neck. This prompted Tarzan to jump out as well. This reduced the pressure on the sides of the dinghy and highlighted just how much air had been lost. Michael told me to hang onto Tarzan's collar so that Tarzan could help drag us to shore. After what seemed like an age we reached the shore, my face wet with tears. It would be years later that I would discover that the dinghy was not leaking: Michael had let the air out to make our day more exciting.

This incident certainly motivated me to actually learn to swim. Up to this point I had done everything I could to avoid it. Before swim classes at school, I would pull the cord in my bathers so that I would spend the lesson rethreading the cord rather than in the pool. When I did get in the pool, I would watch the teacher and walk when they were not looking or drag myself along the edge or the lane ropes. But after the terrifying lake incident, I was committed to learning rather than cheating.

My parents also kept their promise of giving me an electric train set once they were convinced that I had permanently stopped sucking my thumb. Advised by the local school teacher, who was a train enthusiast, it was an 'N' gauge set and was installed on a board that was six by four feet. The reason I recall the dimensions so well was a comment by the school teacher which led me to do a good deal of mental arithmetic. His own train set was on a five by five foot board. As the circumference was the same, I casually said that they were the same size, but he proudly claimed that his was bigger, because the area was bigger. Something in the way he said that irritated me, and so I set about finding a rectangle that would have the same circumference and be bigger. I did not achieve it, but I did invent some maths of my own in the process – which is not to say that someone else had not done this well before I did.

What I discovered in my trial and error is that the multiple of two numbers either side of a squared number is always one less than the square. For example, five by five is 25, four by six is 24. When I stretched this further, to be two numbers away from the square, the difference was always four. So, the area efficiency of a rectangle is always the square of the difference the two sides are away from a square. In the trainset example, a one by nine table would have the same circumference but would have an area 16 fewer than the square: $X^2 - 1 = (X+1)(X-1)$, and $X^2 - Y^2 = (X+Y)(X-Y)$

Beyond the maths, the trainset also provided my family with a focus for gift giving for years. By the time the board was placed vertically on the wall, it had accumulated multiple trains, tracks, buildings, landscapes, people, animals, and cars – all to scale. Adjusting it to cater for the changes was possibly more fun than playing with it.

Deb Beats the Odds

It was around the middle of grade six that we all got collected early from school to take Deb to the doctor. Early that day her world had turned upside down, literally. She had been walking along at school when she blinked and the path became the sky and the sky the path. Disorientated, she sat down, and her friend helped her to the school nurse. Mum was then called to collect her and us from school.

Later that day she would be diagnosed with brain cancer, and that night she would be admitted to hospital in Melbourne for emergency surgery. The doctor gave her a 5% chance of surviving the operation and, if she did survive, she was given an 80% chance of being paralysed down one side of her body, possibly both. If she did not have the surgery, she would be unlikely to live for more than six weeks. Faced with this diagnosis my parents asked Deb what she wanted to do. She thought it was obvious – she would have the surgery.

Barb, Cindy, and I were unaware of any of this. We were left in the car outside the doctor's office in Ballarat to be woken many hours later, after day had turned to night, by an ex-neighbour Mr Cobb. He told us that my parents had gone to Melbourne in an ambulance with Debbie and that we would be staying with his family that night.

It was an awkward night. We had no clothes other than what we were wearing. The Cobbs were trying hard to be nice to us, but we also sensed that they pitied us in some way. I don't recall the evening meal, but I do remember the breakfast being lumpy porridge. They dropped us at school the next day and said that we would be able to go home and get some things after school for the next night. The day started with the whole school being in Chapel, and everyone prayed for Deb together. It was during this gesture that it really struck me how serious things were. During the day, we still had no news about Deb.

At the end of the school day, we were picked up by Tony's mum and taken home to get clothes, toiletries and other essentials, then taken to Tony's house. It was a relief for me as this was my second home, but it was uncomfortable for my sisters who hardly new Tony's sisters. Still there was no news of Deb, and dinner was very subdued. That night I remember hearing one of my sisters crying.

The next day we went to school again. At some point during that day, we were told that Deb had survived the surgery and was in recovery. The following day, the headmaster told us that he was going to Melbourne, so he would be able to give us a lift to the hospital to see our sister (I found out weeks later that he only went to Melbourne for us). We did not get to see Deb for long, she was having an allergic reaction to something (turned out to be penicillin) and was taken into the emergency room. It was nice to see her and Mum and Dad, but it was a quiet drive home. The headmaster was genuinely nice and tried to cheer us up, but we were not really up for it. We stayed with Tony's family for the rest of the school week, and then Dad picked us up and we stayed in a hotel in Melbourne for the weekend so we could visit Deb.

She was not really up for visitors, and so I spent most of my time exploring the hospital. After a couple of days she was able to smile, although her head was still wrapped in bandages, and she was puffed up like a balloon from her allergic reaction. The good news was that she had full use of her hands and feet. The 28-hour brain surgery had been a success, more so than they had expected.

After the weekend, we went home with Dad, while Mum stayed in Melbourne with Deb, living with her mother (the one who cooked for the shearers) for the few hours each day she was not with Deb. This would go on for many weeks. Having Dad in charge of the house turned out to be a whole new experience.

Dad was always an easy touch for two things – new gadgets, and bulk buying. Without Mum in the house, he was responsible for ensuring we were fed, and his approach was unconventional. Fortunately, lots of families kept dropping by with casseroles and similar meals so that we were not entirely reliant on his efforts in the kitchen. It was not that he could not cook, he had often cooked for us over the years. The problem was that he was now trying new things without much thought to the context of his attempts.

One of his early attempts was to start cooking a roast after we had arrived home well after our normal mealtime. By the time it was cooked he had to wake us up to feed it to us. This may have been the inspiration for his purchase of a giant pressure cooker, which promised to cook everything in a third of the time. The problem with this was that he struggled to get the internal barriers to work, so the contents of the various compartments leaked into each other wrecking multiple meals. He eventually did away with the dividers and created a series of giant stews that we would eat over several days.

The meal we hated most though was the Brussels sprouts. Dad had gone to the wholesale fruit and vegetable market that morning and got excited about a 10 kg fresh bag of Brussels sprouts. He was keen to share them with us while they were still fresh, so keen he forgot to cook anything else with them. So even though he had only cooked half of them in the pressure cooker, we each received a full bowl of nothing but Brussels sprouts. I hated Brussels sprouts, and so did my sisters. We ate as many as we could stomach and made our excuses to leave the rest.

The next day Tony's mum came to drop off another round of casseroles and puddings (we loved her puddings). While she was inside talking to Dad, I snuck what remained of the Brussels sprouts into the back of her car. Unfortunately, the bag was spotted before she drove away and so we had to endure the dreaded vegetable with most meals for the next week. By then, even Dad had had enough of them.

On weekends we would go and visit Deb. She got less puffy quickly although not back to her normal shape, and eventually the bandages were removed to reveal a massive C-shaped scar on the back of her head where they had opened her skull to access her brain. They had shaved this part of her head, and soon after Deb would shave the rest of her head so that it would all grow back about the same length. What she was not expecting was that the hair over the part of her skull that they had opened-up would grow back curly while the rest of her hair remained straight.

After a few weeks she was able to leave hospital as a kind of day patient, where she had to return regularly for treatment. During this time, she lived with cousins David and Sarah in Hawthorn. My aunt and uncle also set up a room for my parents to sleep in while Deb was there. On weekends there were folding beds for Cindy, Barb and I in the room next to the kitchen that we put out at night and packed up in the morning. The whole family were incredibly supportive, and if they resented the massive interruption to their lives, they have never mentioned it.

Unfortunately, poor Deb was tired most of the time, and for an energetic younger brother accustomed to having his big sister as his most willing accomplice in any mischief, this was a major downer. Also given it was a suburban house, there seemed to be nothing to do. One thing I do remember doing was shaving – not that I had any facial hair. But I was in my aunt and uncles' bathroom, and he had a blade razor, while Dad had always used an electric one. So, I put on some shaving cream and started shaving, which was when I noticed my uncle was watching me from the door with a wry grin on his face. He was not in the house much when we were awake and spoke to us kids even less. So, I recall the instant clearly as I was worried about how he was going to react. I need not have worried – as soon as I spotted his presence he turned and left.

While we were worried about Deb, Dad was also worried about his father who had been diagnosed with intestinal cancer. I think this was generally kept from us kids, because we did not hear much about it. Perhaps it was because Pop, Dad's father, was a private man. While I knew him longer and spent more time with him than my maternal grandfather, I cannot recall him speaking much. He was always neatly dressed, slightly more formal as was the manner of his generation. His most striking feature was the one we were not to talk about. He only had one hand. The other hand had been badly damaged in an industrial accident, which eventually resulted in it being amputated just below the elbow. He always wore a shirt, tie and jacket, and the sleeve on the arm with the absent hand was neatly folded and pinned up on the outside of his forearm. Pop also had a unique eating implement. It was a knife and fork in one, with the curve of the blade extended around into the fork at the end, not dissimilar to a cheese knife.

Having spent six weeks with one arm in a sling after an operation on my shoulder in my early thirties, I can only imagine how difficult life must have been for him. I don't recall him ever complaining, it was not something that generation ever seemed to do. They always reflected that there were many people that had things much worse than they did, which leant perspective.

To try and help lift Dad's spirits, and perhaps the rest of us, it was decided to give Dad a birthday party. I remember putting up the decorations in my aunt's dining room the night before.

Unfortunately, the party was not to be. Pop died overnight, and Dad was a very sad man on his birthday.

Looking back on these events as a parent of three and having lost my own father, I am in awe of my parents' resilience during this time. Their ability to love and support all of us and each other as they negotiated their own uncertainty, helpless to change the fate of those they loved, was remarkable. Not for a second in my entire life have I ever doubted my parents' love for me. It has been something that I have tried to give to my own children.

Being very different people, my parents' coping methods were also very different. Mum tended to plan and worry, whereas Dad tried to live in the now and laugh. This is possibly why he decided to take us to the drive-in cinema to see *One Flew Over the Cuckoo's Nest* while Mum and Deb were still in Melbourne. I am not sure how well planned the excursion was, but we went in Mum's Mini. On the way in Dad decided to drive over all the row-ramps where cars propped for viewing, which with the Mini's short wheel-base and proximity to the ground felt like a carnival ride. This feeling was enhanced by Dad laughing, and then the rest of us joining in. We also managed to laugh through most of the movie – when I watched it years later, I was surprised to find how serious the undertones were. But that was Dad, life was to be enjoyed, even in the face of pain and hardship.

Mum and Deb eventually came home, but everything was somehow different. Not in any way we could put a finger on, it was just different. Many years later, when we were both adults, Deb would ask me very seriously, 'Did I change? Was my personality different after the operation?' After I repeatedly assured her that she hadn't changed, I finally asked her why she thought she might have. Her reply was chilling, 'Because, except for you, everyone treated me differently.'

This was not necessarily all bad, as Deb reflected on her dread of going back to school with her wig-hair, and navigating the school buses. She need not have worried. Even the toughest of the kids on the bus were on her side. Anyone who was unaware of what she had been through and wanted to draw attention to her wig, or her struggles to navigate steps (Deb lost a significant amount of her peripheral vision), was put in their place if they dared to make a disparaging comment.

At the time of writing, over forty years later, Deb is still living independently having recently retired. To put this in sharp contrast, her roommate during her early weeks in hospital had a similar operation and was given better odds. She sadly did not survive another 12 months. Since her illness, Deb has faced many challenges, some of which I will cover in later chapters. I have never heard her complain about her struggles. It is my strong belief that her attitude is one of the main reasons she has beaten the odds.

Family Pets

One of the other things that helped Deb to cope was a milking cow, which she named Annabelle after one of her school friends. Annabelle would later be joined by another smaller milking cow named Weanie after another of her school friends. The idea was a suggestion from her brain surgeon, I think it was intended as some sort of tactile therapy – it was certainly an activity Deb enjoyed. She would rise before the sun to bring the cows in for milking before she returned to the house to get ready for school. Then she would be back out there after school and on weekends as part of her daily routine.

But the milking cows were not the only pets we had, nor the strangest. Annabelle's presence helped to enable Cindy to have a pet calf, which she called George. It was the first of her pets she was able to cuddle. Until this point, she had been given various birds as pets. At one point, part of the disused chicken shed had been refitted to create a walk-in aviary for budgies. When they were no longer with us, it was converted to house two peacock chicks, until they eventually grew strong enough wings to fly and then they wandered freely. In summer they would perch in the pine trees, but in winter they liked sitting on the bonnet of the car after it had been driven, probably because it was warm, as well as being out of reach of the rats. Unfortunately, they often relieved themselves on departure and people would comment on the fact that we must have very big chooks.

The first pet I remember us getting was a corgi, which was given to Debbie for her birthday when we were still in the old house. She called it Cuddles, and as the only pet in the house Cuddles got a lot of affection from four small kids. Outside the house the sheep dogs played a little rougher. Fortunately, Cuddles found ways to get away from them, using her lack of legs to go through holes in fences that they could not fit through. She also accompanied us kids when we wandered the farm. I think our parents thought she would help alert us to snakes. Certainly, she liked chasing rabbits, and the cows liked chasing her.

Cindy got her budgies at about the same age that Deb had been given Cuddles, and when it came to be my turn for a pet, I was given a labrador puppy. It came with the name the breeder gave it, which I unfortunately don't recall. The reason for this is that I had the puppy less than two weeks when it got out and Dad backed over it with the car. I remember him crying as he told me the news. Other than crying from laughing too much, which he did frequently, Dad did not cry often. My first puppy was soon replaced by another called Chelsea, who would live long enough to have puppies of her own, sired by one of the sheep dogs. She would eventually die from eating a poison bait put out by one of the neighbours. That was after many happy times playing in the wet, as Chelsea loved water.

We also hand reared lambs and calves that had been orphaned or abandoned by their mothers. They were generally kept in the pens in the shearing shed until they were large enough to start eating grass, when they were put in the paddock behind the sheds which we called the '18 Acres'. We would then bang on a bucket when we had prepared the powdered milk ready to feed them and they would come running up to be fed. We tried not to get emotionally attached to any of them as we knew that they would soon be going to market. There were two exceptions – a lamb called 'Little One' and a calf called 'George'. In both cases Cindy would become overly attached to them and plead for them to be kept as forever pets.

Little One lasted long enough that she tormented the then very elderly sheep dog James by refusing to be intimidated by him. Given that James had been trained never to bite a sheep, this bravado from a young lamb was very baffling to him, and combined with some arthritis, it ruined him as a sheep dog. Little One was eventually given to a neighbour's flock of sheep, and then became indistinguishable from them.

Unfortunately for George, he was a boy, and despite Cindy's pleas, not good enough to be a bull. He was also quickly too big to be wandering around the yard. So much later than the others, he too would join the rest of his kind, in his case the steers. Not that this stopped Cindy giving him special attention. She would feed him bananas, but not before she had peeled them. She would hand feed him the peel then the fruit wherever she came across him. Eventually he went to market with the other steers.

I am not sure which came first – Cindy's strong attachment to furry animals, or my parents' unwillingness to give her a furry pet – but they both used the other as the justification for their behaviour. No matter the cause, it would eventually be the ruination of Rick as a sheep dog. Rick arrived as a puppy after James died, at around the time that sheep returned to the farm, when I was a teenager. Where Shep and James had been well trained by Dad prior to having kids, Rick got less sheep dog training and lots of affection from Cindy.

While it was clear he had the instinct and athleticism to be a sheep dog, what was less certain was his mental state. When asked to jump onto the back of the Landcruiser he would sometimes jump onto the bonnet. When driving he would sometimes leap off to chase its shadow. Worst of all was when herding the sheep, he would ignore commands, snap at the sheep and occasionally split the flock. These were all danger signs.

When it came to the actual sheep work, Rick was unreliable. He liked chasing things, which was fine if the sheep that were moving the most were the ones you wanted him to get back, but sometimes it meant that he ran around to the front of where you were trying to go and herded them back to you. Out of desperation, I would throw whatever I could pick up in the direction I wanted him to go. This worked for a while, until I hefted a large rock and he picked up on the shadow rather than the airborne rock. Unfortunately, when rock and shadow met, Rick was in between. Not that it stopped him. I should have known better, as he had done the same thing to a stunt-kite my aunt had given me for my birthday. After numerous tries, I was getting a handle on how to make it climb, swoop and dive, all the time Rick was enjoying chasing its shadow – then it swooped close to the ground and Rick ran right through it, destroying it.

Farm dogs are often let loose around the house during the day if people are home, they tend to stay nearby. Rick was no exception; he would join in with Cuddles the corgi at greeting visiting cars by barking at them as they came and went as well as follow us as we did our various chores and errands. Certainly, Cindy made little distinction between Rick and Cuddles in the way she treated them, other than Rick was not allowed inside the house.

Unfortunately, I was the one that discovered that Rick had gone down the paddocks and attacked some sheep. I was driving the old tractor with a trailer on the back when I saw him running among the sheep. Fortunately, he came when I called him, but when he arrived, I noticed his face was bloody. I took him onto the back of the trailer and tied him up by the collar, then drove over to check on the sheep. He had killed some of them. Others were badly wounded. I had to put several of them out of their misery. It was a horrible day, one that Rick would not live to see the end of. Even Cindy agreed that he had to be put down.

After that day I became the farm's sheepdog. I would ride on the sideboard of the Landcruiser so I could leap-off while it was still moving, run after the sheep and leap back on again. I was nowhere near as athletic as a dog, but at least I always did the right thing.

Rick was not the last dog we had. Eventually Barb would get a puppy, and I would also be given one at the same time, to keep it company. This time around Mum decided we were getting cocker spaniels. They were soft, cuddly, dumb, and completely unsuitable for a farm. By this time, we had two acres of open lawn between the house and the school. Most mornings there would be rabbits happily feasting on the abundance of green grass, particularly in summer when all around were parched paddocks. These two dogs, Judy and Sarah, were very keen on hunting rabbits. But they did it almost entirely with their noses. We would watch them hunt the rabbits by scent as the rabbits watched them and casually hopped away to eat grass in a different spot, sometimes where the dogs had just been. I think even the elderly Cuddles was baffled by their incompetence, she would occasionally join in to show them how it was done, but the rabbits were too fast, and the spaniels too stupid.

In addition to their inability to learn, they also had naturally long coats that needed to be trimmed and webbed feet that collected burrs. The farmer's solution to this was to shave them short and often. What they were good at was swimming. We would stretch out on floating devices and hold their collars as they dragged us around the dam. Regardless of their unsuitability for country life, we loved them dearly and gave them lots of affection.

The strangest and least affectionate pets we had were the goats. I have no idea where the inspiration came from, but there were originally four of them, one each, when I was in early primary school. Three females and a male, the male was given to me, and I unimaginatively named him Billy. Even on arrival he was as tall as me and cantankerous. Over time he would grow a very long set of horns, a long coat, and a foul odour. As unpleasant and unappealing as he was as a pet, he must have charmed the female goats, because the herd grew quickly.

What they did not do was behave. They got through fences so readily that we stopped pretending to put them in various paddocks and just dealt with them where we found them. Part of this problem was that they also made gaps in fences for others to follow. Within a few years, Dad had enough and decided to sell them. Rounding them up was not easy, we had to round up a herd of cattle with them, using the cattle to surround them and run them into the cattle yards. From there they were loaded onto a fenced trailer and taken to a neighbour's clearing sale to be sold.

But this was not the end of them. They escaped from their new owners who lived some distance away and returned to our farm two weeks later. We rounded them up again and took them back to their new owners. They found their way to our farm again, and this time they were returned minus Billy – who was blamed for their escape antics and smelt so bad that they didn't like having him around anyway. I think the plan was to sell Billy separately, but after numerous failed attempts to catch him, and ongoing damage to fences, Billy was eventually shot.

I remember it clearly as I still had some emotional attachment to him despite his bad temper and foul odour. We had managed to corner him not too far from the tip, and Dad was taking an age to line up the shot from about 30 metres away, while Billy stared us down. I recall hoping that it would be a clean shot and fortunately for Billy it was. The odds certainly were against it.

Shots in the Night

Billy and Rick were not the only animals on the farm to exit this world via the wrong end of a gun, although all the others I can remember were rabbits. My grandmother told stories of rabbits being in plague proportions on her parents' farm in her childhood. She said that when they had fenced the perimeter with rabbit-proof fencing and driven the remaining rabbits together, that they were so numerous as to resemble a flock of sheep, and she had even caught one between her legs when it had tried to escape.

Rabbits were not as problematic in my childhood, although at various times they were more plentiful than others. So it was that at irregular intervals a night of spotlight shooting would be arranged. Spotlight shooting was a relatively simple concept: nocturnal animals, like rabbits, confronted by a bright light, have a tendency to stop and stare at the light – which makes them easier to shoot. On our farm spotlighting generally had three people on the back and two in the cabin of the Landcruiser. The three on the back would stand facing over the cabin, with a shooter either side, and the person pointing the spotlight in the middle. In the cabin would be the driver and the dogsbody, whose job it was to open the gates, and to fetch the shot rabbits. This was my job from early primary school age, sometimes shared with my sisters.

Shooting was not just a farm activity in the 1970s. We frequently had to tell people wandering around with guns on the farm that they were trespassing and were required to leave. It never occurred to me as a child driving up to a stranger armed with a gun and telling them that they had to go that I was in any danger of being shot. What we were more concerned about was being shot because they had not seen us, or having farm animals shot intentionally or accidentally. We had heard stories of a farmer's prize bull being shot and the head taken as a trophy – it may have been a rural myth, but we did not want it happening to us. The only people permitted to wander the farm were Murray and Len, and we were not at all worried about being shot by them as they never seemed to fire their guns.

That there were two lawyers who owned guns and went shooting was no big deal. Nor was it a surprise that the local primary teacher and the electrician did the same. Shooting was like fishing, just something some people did on the weekend, while other people thought it was either not for them or mean to the animals. It was the primary school teacher who owned the bloodhound that was one of first shooters I met. After he moved away, the most regular shooter was the electrician who worked on the house. I have forgotten his name, but I recall that he was one of the first men I knew with long hair – and that he was relaxed, good company and a particularly good shot. Unfortunately, Dad was not a good shot.

Dad owned two guns – a 22 rifle with a telescopic sight, and a five shot automatic shot gun. Both were kept in his study. The day before a scheduled spotlighting session the 22 rifle would be taken out and we would go down near the tip for shooting practice and to ensure the sights were properly adjusted. With Dad these were two incompatible activities. He would regularly miss the target (stuck on the back of a wrecked car), after several attempts at this he would adjust the sights, then repeat the process. Sometimes this resulted in him getting closer to the target, often it did not. On bad days he would resort to getting Mum to come down to see if she could do better. She always could. Mum was a very reliable shot, but she did not like shooting. Within two or three shots she would have the scope adjusted correctly, and then hit the target consistently, before handing the gun back, job done. When I got older, I took over from Mum, although it took me a little longer. The first shot was always interesting to see just how far askew the sights would be. When they were correctly adjusted it was like a magic trick to squeeze the trigger and have a hole appear on the target some distance away.

Spotlight shooting was ideally done on clear moonless nights, when the grass was not too long. This combination generally resulted in it also being a cold night. It was one of the reasons I did not mind being in the cabin. The night generally started with the shooters taking turns on who would shoot, but would quickly become a call on whether it was likely to be a dinner shot or not. If it was a dinner shot, then the shooter other than Dad would take the shot. A dinner shot simply meant that the rabbit was presenting in a way that it could be cleanly shot (ideally in the head) without damaging the edible parts of the rabbit. Dad could not be relied on for dinner shots. I liked it when they managed a good dinner shot, because it also meant that the rabbit would not still be alive when I went to collect them. I had to break the necks on those that were still alive, and it was not something I enjoyed.

Fortunately, Mum has some great rabbit recipes, and we all enjoyed the weeks after spotlighting, particularly a dish called Mrs Raymond – named after the person who had given Mum the recipe. The dogs also enjoyed having a rabbit diet, although they often also had to deal with buckshot and broken bones. This was because without fail, well before the end of a spotlighting night, Dad would have given up on the rifle and taken up the shotgun. Even then he sometimes needed several shots to hit each rabbit. This lack of precision is why I was so relieved he managed to shoot straight for Billy the goat.

I only used the shotgun once. I am left-handed, and the automatic discharge of the cartridge came out the right side of the gun across the bridge of my nose. I was also never one of the shooters on spotlighting night. This was because I was too short to comfortably stand behind the cabin and point the gun toward the ground at the front.

I did go spotlighting with another school friend, Ben, on a trip to his farm toward the end of grade six. Ben was a boarder and lived on a rice farm east of Deniliquin. His parents were divorced, and I never met his mother. I remember his dad picking us up from school at the start of the Melbourne Cup long weekend in a V8 Ford ute with a large bull-bar on the front. The cabin had a bench seat and we sat three across with me in the middle. It was a four-hour drive and we stopped for dinner along the way and then drove into the night with the road disappearing beneath us at rapid rate, as we were travelling well over the speed limit.

We arrived in the dark to a cold house and immediately went to bed. I awoke in the morning to a house very similar to the one from my early childhood, although with fewer creature comforts. This was a dwelling used for sleeping and eating and little more as from dawn till dusk, and probably later Ben's dad was elsewhere on the farm. Their most prized possession was the largest tractor I had ever seen. It had a white airconditioned cabin complete with sound system that was positioned in the middle of four equally large wheels. The other thing about the tractor was that it pivoted in the middle, beneath the cabin. The equipment it pulled around was equally oversize compared to our farm. At home the plough (farm equivalent of a shovel) and scarifier (farm equivalent of multiple headed hoe) were not much wider than the tractor. Here, these attachments were at least 20 metres across. The other large piece of machinery was the header, which is used to harvest the rice crop. Ben's Dad said that the tractor and header were worth more than the farm. I had no idea if this was true or not, but I believed him.

The farm itself was completely flat, except for the raised farm roads and irrigation channels. Most of the farm was bare as the crops had been harvested, the stubble cleared, and the ploughing was yet to begin. Ben and I spent the first part of the day driving an old car around at high speed, getting it to drift across the dusty landscape. The day warmed quickly under a baking sun. After lunch we decided to go swimming in one of the main irrigation channels between Ben's farm and the neighbours. This was something I only agreed to after Ben assured me that the water was warm. The channels were concrete lined and had regular barriers across them to control the height of the water. Upstream of these barriers the water was higher, with the water flowing over the barrier like a waterfall. Above the barrier was a narrow walkway. We swam by diving off the walkway upstream and allowing the flow of the water to drift us back to the barrier, before climbing up to jump again.

Next to where we were swimming was the neighbour's sunflower crop. The flowers were in full bloom and buzzing with bees. We played hide-and-seek amongst the sunflowers which were at my head height and Ben's shoulder height. When we got back to the house, Ben's Dad asked if we had seen any tiger snakes, which was when I found out that these deadly snakes enjoy swimming on the surface of the warm irrigation channels.

That night we went spotlighting, without guns. One of the things that has always interested me about visiting other people's houses and farms is discovering the little differences in how things are done. Spotlighting at Ben's farm involved him driving while I tried to spotlight a rabbit or anything else. When I found something, Ben would then try and chase it down in the car. We never succeeded in catching anything. As the driving got more reckless, my ability to find anything with the spotlight diminished considerably and intentionally, until we decided to call it a night and go back to the house.

The next day we went to visit Ben's paternal Grandmother in Hay, which was several hours away. We travelled in the ute, via Deniliquin. On the way through Deniliquin Ben's dad was pointing out various landmarks, like the rice silos and the sale yards when a dog ran out to bark at the car. I was sitting on the left side, and I thought we had hit the dog, but Ben and his dad continued talking about the landmarks so I thought I must have been mistaken.

On the drive from Deniliquin to Hay the irrigation country gives way to salt-bush country, a flat semi-arid expanse of sand and salt-bush – a plant not much higher than long grass. A few years later, in year 9, another boarder at school would inherit 50 km^2 of this type of land. When I asked him what he was going to do with it, he said he was going to put sheep on it. I don't recall the exact number, but I do remember it was about the same number as we had on our farm, which was less than 100th of the size. When I asked him about the cost of fencing such a large area for so few sheep, he said that they were not going to fence it. They would just ensure that all of the water wells were away from the boundaries so that the sheep would keep returning to the middle.

Hay was a nice town as I recall it, and Ben's grandmother's house was elegant and expansive. We spent the day playing table tennis and pool, with the larger and more experienced Ben winning every game. After dinner we got back in the ute to head home, which was when we discovered that the left headlight was missing. It turns out we had hit the dog in Deniliquin.

I don't remember what we did on the Sunday, but that night Ben and I were given tickets to see a movie, while Ben's dad had dinner with a woman, I assume it was kind of a date. The night did not go to plan. As the opening credits rolled on *Death on the Nile*, Ben and I lit our cigarettes. I am not sure why we thought this was a good idea, because it turned out to be a very bad idea. Not only did our parents forbid us from smoking, but the cinema did not permit smoking either. We were promptly ejected from the cinema. We spent some time debating whether to spend the next 90 minutes hiding somewhere and then pretend we had seen the movie, but the choice was taken away from us when a friend of the family saw Ben and asked what we were doing. After a slow walk to the RSL Club where Ben's dad was having dinner, we confessed what we had done. His dad was super mad, mainly about having his date wrecked, I think. He made us go and sit in the car and think about what we had done while he thought about our punishment. I was never invited back to Ben's farm. Although, in part, this might have been because we were not in the same class in year 7, which was the start of high school and when the number of kids in the year level more than tripled.

Fighting Over a Girl

There were three year 7 classes, which the school named A, B and C. I was in A and Michael was in B. But the biggest difference was that A was located in the school building near the junior headmaster's office, while B and C were located in the portables between the junior school and the tuckshop, overlooking the back of the swimming pool. It meant that the kids in class A saw much less of the other two classes than those classes saw of each other.

In one of those classes was a new kid called David who had some mental health issues. His condition was made considerably worse if he ate certain foods – like Twisties, red cordial and lollies. Unfortunately for him, some of the boys in those classes found out about these foods and would then feed them to him to see what happened next. Then if David failed to entertain, they would give him ideas.

In class A our little bubble was set on an entirely different course. Some girls in the class were keen on boys, and then not satisfied with finding boys for themselves, set about matchmaking. For teenagers in the '70s dating was often negotiated via intermediaries. This was how I managed to obtain my first official girlfriend. I don't recall how far through the year we were, but we were in winter uniform. I remember being in the classroom when Liz asked me if I liked Cathy. Until that point in time, I was not even sure who Cathy was, but when she was pointed out to me, sitting on one of the desks at the side of the room and watching us sheepishly, I replied that I did. Liz then said that I should ask her out because she liked me too. I don't recall asking her, but we were then going out. I really did not know what that required of me.

That night I asked Deb what I was meant to do, and she said that I had to be extra nice to her and stick up for her if anyone was mean to her. Also, that I should never kiss and tell. Before the week was out, Liz had coordinated excursions to the more secluded parts of the school for the pairs of kids that were going out. This annoyed the other kids.

Not that this was an everyday event. Most days we spent recess and lunch playing kick-to-kick, with boys and girls combined into two big packs with two or three balls launched back and forth between them. Kick-to-kick was a way of playing Australian rules football without the tackling. The ball would be kicked from one end and those at the other would try and mark it (catch the ball), the successful recipient would then kick the ball to the other end where the process would be repeated. The only difference that dating made was that I was now 'waxing' with Cathy. Waxing was when you tried to kick to the advantage of that person at the other end. Given that both of our kicks were unreliable, it made little difference. The two best kicks were girls. Like a lot of the girls at that age, they were also taller than most of the boys.

It might surprise some younger readers that given there would be no female football league for another generation, the girls and boys played sport together. This was commonplace, while the television shows and advertisements were overtly sexualised, as kids we always had a mix of male and female friends and a healthy disregard for gender roles. In the 80's a person's sexual preference or identity was never discussed, except for the pop singer Boy George.

Within a couple of weeks of going out with Cathy, another message was delivered to me by Michael. David wanted to fight me. Given I hardly knew him, I asked why. I was told that it was because David did not think it was fair that the shortest kid in the class should be going out with one of the best-looking girls. David was much bigger than me and I had flashbacks of being beaten to a pulp by a bigger kid when I was in Prep because he was keen on one of the girls that I was friends with. I said I did not want to fight, but Michael assured me that he and Ben who were the two largest boys in the class would protect me, so I agreed to fight.

The logic of fighting over girls has always eluded me. I have always thought that it was up to the girl who she wanted to be with. Fighting for a girl as though she was some sort of prize has always struck me as very disrespectful to the girl. With this in mind, I figured that the sort of girl that would choose the smallest boy, was unlikely to change her mind when a bigger and weirder kid beat him up.

The fight was set for a lunchtime in one of the boys change rooms. Every boy in the year level other than me seemed to be excited about it. I was just hoping that Michael and Ben would keep their word before I got badly hurt. I remember standing facing David between two rows of seats and hanging racks with little space to move. I don't recall how the fight started, but I remember ducking as David swung his fist hard at my head. I then bobbed up and punched him hard in the nose. He swung back the other way, I ducked again, bobbed up and punched him again. This was repeated a few more times before someone yelled that a teacher was coming, and the fight was declared over with me as the winner. I had come out unscathed, although if any of the blows had hit, I would have been seriously hurt. I was also acutely aware that nether Michael nor Ben had made any move to protect me. When I confronted them about this, they said that they would have if he had hit me, which given the power he was trying to hit me with, and the hard surfaces all around, would probably have been too late.

The irony of it all was that about six weeks later when Cathy 'dumped' me, the reason she gave was that I was too short. Given that she had not grown any taller, nor I any shorter, this did not make a lot of sense to me. Truth was she, like most of the girls in the year level, had taken a fancy to 'Macca', a boy in one of the other classes, although I don't recall them going out. Six weeks was one of the longer relationships in early high school. Cathy also managed to set the record for the shortest one.

In year 8 one of the boys that also caught the school bus had asked Cathy out at the end of the school day. She had said yes, and when he got on the bus a few minutes later he shared his newfound status to the bus at large and strutted down the aisle like he had just won the world heavy weight championship. It was then pointed out that Cathy was trying to get his attention through the bus window. He made his way over to the window still on cloud nine, only to be told that she had thought about it and didn't want to go out with him after all. It was like watching a balloon deflate, much to the amusement of the whole bus.

The fight was not my last encounter with David. He was key to me being caned on my birthday later that year. The lead up to this was a gradual escalation in hostility toward the birthday boy by the other boys in the year level. Once again, class A was largely protected from this due to its proximity to the staff room and junior headmaster's office. But at some time shortly before my birthday in early August, it became the thing to do to dust the birthday kid with talcum powder. Its origin may have come from the boarding houses. Regardless of the source, the fact that I shared my birthday with another boy, who was not particularly popular, resulted in several of the boys conspiring to powder us as we arrived for school on our birthday.

David's key part in this plot was that he had emptied his family's bathroom, laundry and possibly storage cupboards of all powders – talcum powders, perfumed, foot, cleaning and so on. These had then been distributed among about a dozen boys. The bus always arrived at school close to the start of the first class, and so they had already powdered the other boy before the bus arrived. This was evident in the powder on the ground and the boys gathering like a lynch mob as the bus arrived.

Having dealt with exiting the bus on snow days, I had a plan. To give this some context, on the rare day that it snowed in Ballarat, kids threw snowballs at one another. The problem was when your bus arrived at the bus exchange, the kids getting off the bus had no snowballs, while the mob of kids waiting for the bus to arrive were fully armed. The best tactic in these situations was to get off quickly, get armed and fight back. This was to be my plan. I was helped in its execution by my sisters who offered to take my bag.

So as the bus doors opened, I sprinted off it toward the nearest powder holder, wrenched the powder free and chased after my adversaries. This at least cleared a path off the bus for the other kids, although it did not prevent some of them from having some powder land on them. The result of this mayhem was a lot of kids got powder-coated, which triggered an inquisition by the school. The first hour of the day had kids being called into the headmaster's office to give their version of events. Then various kids were called back to receive their punishment – with the punishment of the day being the cane, ranging from one to 12 hits.

Two of the Michaels who were regular recipients of the cane, prepared for their call-back by putting a few sheets of writing paper down the back of their pants. Inspired by this David put a textbook down the back of his pants – which was clearly visible. This was one of the main reasons he got twelve after the book was spotted and removed. My friend Michael also got twelve, not because the paper was spotted, but because he laughed when the other Michael was being caned as it resulted in puffs of dust coming off with each strike. The other birthday boy did not get caned because he had not fought back, while I got caned because I had 'actively participated'.

The inquisition and punishments put an end to birthday kids being met with hostilities. At the end of the year a new friend of mine, Joe, invited me and three other boys to his birthday celebrations. Joe was a boarder whose parents lived on a farm in western Victoria. He was also one of the few kids younger than me. He had not started school early like me, he had 'skipped' a grade. What this meant was that his primary school teachers had decided that he was smart enough to do the higher year level, and moved him into it. While this was relatively rare, the opposite was quite common; numerous kids would be kept down to repeat the school year if they were not doing well enough. This combination was part of what created the characters of the big dumb kid and the small smart kid in comics and on TV shows. We certainly had a few examples of these in classes at school.

Joe's birthday was in December, and so his mother decided to pick us all up at the end of the school year and take us to Melbourne where we would spend a couple of days doing fun things like ice-skating, kayaking, and going to the movies. The not so fun part was that we stayed with his grandmother. She lived in a mansion and had a maid that was almost as old as she was. I am not sure when she had last left the building, because her expectations of behaviour were out by half a century. One of these was that we were expected to stand whenever she entered the room, bow our heads, and wish her good morning, afternoon or evening depending on the time of day. Then remain standing, head bowed until she had either left the room, or sat down. Fortunately, late on the first day we found a loophole – if you were asleep, you did not have to do this. I

pretended to be asleep often enough that I recall her commenting –
'Is that boy there always sleeping?'

Circular Summers

Shortly after getting back from Joe's birthday bash, I started earning money for working on the farm. This was not because I had reached a particular age, and I would continue to do unpaid work most of the time. The exception was hay-making work, for which we all got paid by the hour for time spent on the tractor either mowing or raking. I generally did the mowing, Cindy generally did the raking, and Dad always did the bailing.

Haymaking highlighted the utility of the tractor, particularly the array of different connection points at the rear. Working up from the bottom is the towbar, which is usually directly behind the driver's seat, but can be moved and pinned across a 45 degree range. Just above that is the PTO shaft. This is a mechanical shaft that is in line with the engine's power train, and is turned on and off by a lever under the left-hand side of the driver's seat. Either side of this are two hydraulic arms that can be used to raise and lower things attached to them, via another lever under the right of the driver's seat. There is another central static attachment point above the PTO shaft that when used in combination with the arms provides a pivot point to enable grader blades or lifting trays to be raised and lowered in a stable vertical fashion. Further up are two hydraulic hose joints, an in and an out. These can be used to pump hydraulic fluid to any attachment that needs it, the lever for this is also on the right of the driver.

Other things can also be attached to the front of the tractor. We had two tractors, and the older one had a belt drive on the right-hand side of the engine. On our farm this was used to run two things, the saw bench and the irrigation pump. The saw bench was not used after the early '70s – effectively replaced by chainsaws. Given it was an unshielded two metre blade driven by an open belt – it was an accident waiting to happen. The irrigation pump was only run during very dry summers as long as the price of fuel was not prohibitive. When it was decided that it was time to irrigate, the tractor would be driven down the long ramp to the waterhole, then there would be lots of fiddling around until the 20 metre belt was in a straight line between tractor and pump, and the tractor dug in so it would not move. It would stay there and run 24 hours a day for at least two weeks, almost draining the enormous waterhole and turning a parched landscape green. But that would not happen until after haymaking.

Haymaking started in early summer, weather permitting. It was designed to harvest the strong spring growth before the hot summer sun baked it dry and bleached it of nutrients. On our farm you could watch this happen from day to day just as you can watch a tide go out. The green would leave the top of the exposed hills first and slide down them over days before draining out of the valleys like a bath emptying. Not every paddock was suitable for haymaking – some were not flat enough, others did not have good enough pastures.

In the early years, I remember Dad mowing the '87 Acres', which was our best hay paddock. He was using the finger mower. This style of mower has triangular blades on a long shaft, like a mechanical hedge-trimmer. It cuts the grass very cleanly, but has a very low tolerance for obstacles. Watching it cut the grass it is almost graceful, as the cut grass elegantly falls over the back of the blade. By the time I joined in haymaking the 87 Acres had retained its name but lost its size – we had sold most of it as five acre blocks to hobby farmers. We had also sold two other paddocks that had also been used for haymaking as well as the bush block. What they all had in common was they were on the edge of the farm and could not be seen from the house. It meant we needed to find new hay paddocks and use tougher equipment.

The tougher equipment was a twin slasher, with two shafts and three blades per shaft. It was like two oversized and synchronised lawnmowers, with one spinning clockwise and the other anticlockwise, so that the cut grass was blown into a single row out the back of the machine. Because it was so wide, it was required to be towed sideways, and attached to the tractor in the chosen paddock. It was an older machine, and had no safety covers on the PTO shafts. For those unfamiliar with farm machinery, a PTO shaft is very similar to a drive-train on a vehicle. Sometimes you can see them on trucks when at the lights – it is the long spinning bar that goes from the gearbox to the rear axle, usually with a universal joint on either end as this allows flexibility in the angle of attachment at either end.

On the slasher, there were three gearboxes and three PTO shafts. The first shaft attached from the tractor PTO shaft to a gearbox directly behind it, another drive shaft connected that to a gearbox above the first set of blades, and the third shaft connected to the final gearbox above the outer blades. Because the mower was at right angles to the tractor, the slasher was connected to the two hydraulic arms to ensure that it was kept rigid. The arms were not used to adjust the height of the mower. This was done by winding up and down the height of the three wheels.

We had purchased a newer, more powerful tractor to power the slasher, and it had come with a roll-cage as standard, something not equipped on the older tractor. To this, Dad had added a roof and a windscreen. On this tractor I would spend many days going around in circles for hours for the next 10 summers. So, the details are burnt into my memory.

In addition to the size of the equipment, mowing paddocks differs from mowing lawns in one other important way – it is important to avoid cutting the grass twice as it wrecks the hay. It was with this in mind that I would carefully follow the edge of the uncut grass lap after lap, hour after hour. In doing so, I got to know the limits of the equipment – particularly how sharp I could turn the corners, and how to avoid changing gears.

Changing gears was not a simple exercise while mowing, as during mowing the engine had to be running at 2,000 rpm to drive the mower. With the mower speed and power fixed, then gears were used to ensure that the mower did not stall, with lower gears for thicker grass. Because the mower had to be going at full speed before moving forward, the tractor needed to start moving at close to full revs. This was hard on the clutch.

To help cope with the monotony of this we had a set of radio headphones. The only problem was that you needed to turn your head to tune them properly. They were also heavy, particularly after several hours, which is why we wrapped an old sock around the top to pad them. It was in my second year of mowing that this piece of equipment saved my life.

I had been mowing for many hours, and a sharp corner edge of the uncut section was now aligned with a steep slope on the side of a ridge. I was turning the tractor sharply into this when a bolt came loose on the outer arm connecting the tractor to the mower. As a result, the tractor turned in toward the mower, and the mower caught on the tractor tyre lug and started climbing up the back of the tractor. This resulted in the back of the mower blades hitting the ground and flinging rocks and dirt into the cabin space – smashing the windscreen and knocking the headphones off my head. The PTO shaft at the back of the tractor had also come loose and was now spinning wildly behind me. As all this was going on, I pushed the hand throttle lower with my right hand, reached under the left side of my seat and shut off the PTO, turned the tractor away from the mower and slammed on the brakes. I breathed hard, then shut off the engine and pulled on the hand brake. I got out, looked at the destruction, and walked home to tell Dad.

He came to inspect the damage, and when he saw the wreckage and the position of the tractor on the slope, he was visibly shaken. He hugged me tight, told me I must have been very cool headed to respond the way I did and called off work for the day. There is only one other time I remember him calling off work, and it was also a time my reflexes saved my life. The two of us were repairing a gate and I was holding something in place, while Dad swung the sledgehammer at a bolt near the top of the post. Problem was, he missed the post, and the sledgehammer was going to connect with my head. I dropped out of the way, no harm done, but it was close enough for work to stop.

Other than these two isolated incidents, haymaking was very monotonous. The only part of it that was close to fun was raking, because the tractor went a lot faster. Cindy was better at that than me, Dad raved about how consistent her rows were – which was important to him because it meant that he did not have to change gears while baling the hay. We never actually did the hay carting – taking the bales from the paddock and stacking them in the sheds. That is because we had an arrangement with a neighbour, where we did not need to buy hay carting equipment, and they did not need to buy a hay baler. Dad baled their hay and they carted ours, with a payment one way or the other making up the balance.

The order in which everything was done was weather dependent. We would generally start in the dryer paddocks, with the first key deadline to cut the hay while the grass was still green. Then it would be raked shortly afterward so that less of it would be bleached by the sun or damaged by the rain. Sometimes, if there was a long gap between raking and baling, it would be raked again on the eve of baling. Dad always bailed at night, and only as much as they could cart the next day. A hay bale that is rained on becomes compost. A haystack full of wet bales catches fire. The idea of baling at night was that the grass could be drier because the night air stopped the bales from being dusty. It worked well – but it made for a sleepy Dad during the day.

I recall one summer I rode over a red-bellied black snake on my bike near the house. I thought it was a garden hose until it reared up at me. I raced inside and woke Dad up and was very frustrated by how long he took to follow me outside to kill the snake. In the '70s if you saw a snake, you killed the snake – because if you did not, the snake might kill the next person. Red-bellied black snakes are one of the top ten most deadly snakes in the world. Given that this snake was close to the house, I was keen for it not to kill any of our family, friends, or pets. Dad eventually lumbered over to where I had seen the snake, long handled shovel at the ready, but of course the snake was gone. Fortunately, we spotted it between us and the house, and then Dad hit it on the head with the flat of the shovel blade, killing it instantly.

As kids, we had all been told not to cut off the head of a snake, because someone had once, and the head had spun up and bitten him on the neck and killed him. I am not sure if that is true, but certainly we only ever saw adults kill them by belting their heads flat. This was something we also attempted when confronted by a snake on the side of the road just after we had gotten off the school bus one afternoon. Five or six of us surrounded it and threw rocks at it until we had killed it. We also were told that snakes don't like noise, so if we were walking through long grass in the paddocks (often in bare feet) we would talk loudly (even when alone) or hit the ground with a stick to make thumping noises. It might have worked, I never saw a snake while doing this, although I must admit it could feel pretty stupid talking loud nonsense to yourself while walking along. But mostly it was just part of summer.

Another thing that became part of summer from about this time was Dad's mother staying with us for a few weeks.

Gran Kent

Both of my grandmothers were referred to by us as Gran, so to distinguish between them in conversation we added their surname. Gran Kent was a force of nature who would live to be 96, with all her mental faculties intact. The manner of her death is an insight into her robust approach to life.

Gran generally just got on with life and called things as she saw them. So, it was a surprise to the country aged care facility when she declared, while in apparently good health, that she was about to die. She requested that all her children be informed so that she could say goodbye to them. The message was passed on, along with the observation that she appeared to be in good health. Given that only one of her four children lived nearby, it took the others a week or two to make travel arrangements for the visit. My father, accompanied by Deb, was the last to make the trip, after which the two of them had a laugh about it being a false alarm. That night, Gran died peacefully in her sleep from natural causes. Apparently, even death was able to be bent to her will.

Gran was a strong woman, but she also had a good sense of humour and a keen interest in learning about practical things outside the kitchen. In the kitchen she had her own way of doing things that did not readily adapt to the nuances of new equipment. After she had laid waste to several cooking implements and appliances in the relatively new farm kitchen, Mum and Dad had a private discussion.

The result was that I was to invite Gran to accompany me as I did my chores around the farm.

It was the start of a wonderful relationship. I explained to her how to fix fences, what to look for to distinguish between healthy and unhealthy cattle, how to spot a fly-blown sheep and numerous other farm skills that she was never going to use but was intently interested in. In return I would get an incredibly rich first-hand account of the 20th century, all of which was exchanged as we drove around the farm in an un-airconditioned Landcruiser in the middle of multiple summers. If we stopped in one place for too long, for example to fix a hole in a fence, she would get bored and tell me she was going to walk home. I would point her in the right direction, then go and find her when I had finished the task at hand. Often when I found her, she would have collected some quartz rocks with yellow veins on them, which she thought might be gold. They were all worthless. However, what I learnt from her was priceless.

Gran was born in 1901, before cars, phones, radio, TV, washing machines, dish washers, airplanes, and world wars. Her father was a stockbroker who had been part of the initial capital raising of BHP and became the longest serving chairman of the Melbourne Stock Exchange – a position he held through the First World War. Gran would recount how he had closed the stock exchange at the outbreak of the war for a few days. Apparently, he was keen to make sure people did not overreact to the news with speculative trades. It was not a popular decision at the time, but it set a precedent that has been followed globally since. She was very proud of his calm head and commitment to do the right thing, even if it was not the popular thing.

Gran was the youngest of six children, she had four brothers and a sister. Her oldest brother was her favourite and was following in his father's footsteps before he joined the army at the start of the First World War and was killed in action at Gallipoli. Even 60 years later, Gran still shed a tear talking about it. Her second oldest brother also died during the First World War, killed in action on the western front in France. Her third oldest brother was too young for the First World War, but he would fight in the Second World War. He was taken prisoner by the Japanese and worked on the Burmese railway. He returned a changed man. Gran took him into their household and tried to take care of him. My Dad recalls being scared of his yelling in the night, and how he once had Dad's sister by the throat while his mind was clearly somewhere else. Gran just said that the war broke him and that he died soon after he returned. Of her sister she said that she was older, but they didn't get along. And of her younger brother, he was a Doctor in Albany in Western Australia. She described him as kind and gentle, and Albany as a beautiful place.

Gran's mother was born in England. She was the last of my ancestors to arrive in Australia – in 1889, and would return there only once in her life – in the 1920s. It was a trip that Gran would also make. They went by ship, going through the Suez Canal in one direction, and returning via Cape Town on the way home. Some of the stops along the way included India and Egypt. I am not sure what port they stopped at in India – but Gran thought it was a 'dreadful place'. The highlight of her trip was playing golf in Hyde Park in London. Apparently, she saw a man playing and asked if he could teach her, he obliged, and she would play golf as often as she could from that day forward.

I am not sure if Gran's looks had anything to do with the man's willingness to teach her how to play golf. Most people did what Gran wanted. The only photos of a young Gran were her wedding photo, in which she looks fashionably serious, and a photo of her as an actress playing Lady Bracknell in the Oscar Wilde play *The Importance of Being Earnest*. She apparently did it very well, but I am not sure how much was acting and how much was her own personality.

Other than helping to push Gran up into the passenger seat of the Landcruiser, there was no point trying to push Gran to do anything. The harder one tried, the more she resisted. I got her to do lots of things by making her laugh. Gran had an appreciation for mischief. She also enjoyed winning. We would often play cards with her at night, (it helped keep her out of the kitchen), and we often suspected her of cheating. One night the lighting was just right to turn her glasses into mirrors, and my young eyes were good enough to be able to see the cards in her hand. I can't recall the game we were playing but it required certain cards to be presented if prompted. Gran had the card and did not play it. I called her out for cheating. She acted outraged, so I blurted that I could see her cards in her glasses. She thought that was fantastic and laughed for ages.

It was not just with cards that she bent the truth to her will. She had noticed that her local Bowls club were less inclined to select women over 70 for the competitive teams. So, she wrote that she was 68 on her membership form every year for nearly two decades. Gran's body matched her mind in its robust nature. Every now and then, some of my aunts, who were nurses, would suggest she lose some weight. Gran would then declare her diet a success by saying she had gone in several notches on her belt. We found out later she had purchased a larger belt. But the truth bending went up a notch when it came to her dogs.

Gran lived alone in the house in Kew, a suburb of Melbourne, that had been home to the family she raised. It was full of memories, but was poorly suited to an elderly lady as it was situated in a large yard on a steep slope. She only used a few of the rooms and in winter would spend most of the time within two metres of the old gas heater in the lounge room with a rug across her knees. The kitchen was a time capsule from the '40s and the house also had several steps between different rooms. Into this Gran introduced a small dog named Billy. On one occasion when we visited her, Billy ran out of the house and down the street when Gran opened the door to let us in, to which Gran casually observed, 'Billy is taking himself for a walk'. Over about a five-year period I think I saw at least three different dogs, but Gran called them all Billy and acted as though they were the same dog.

Apparently, Gran's approach to life also applied to driving. She was one of the first women in Melbourne to drive a car before a licence was needed, and one of the first to get a licence when that was required. The only car I recall her having was a 1968 Holden Kingswood. It was an automatic which meant that my one-armed grandfather could drive it, although it had no power steering. It was also a bright blue colour. I never witnessed Gran driving, and I am sure she was a better driver in her youth. But shortly after I got my licence, the Police contacted my uncle (Gran's next of kin) and told him that she needed to be taken off the road. When he asked if she had been in an accident they said, 'no, but she keeps causing them'. A plan was hatched. When Gran went in for minor surgery, I was to go to her house (with the car keys given to me by my uncle) and take her car back to our farm.

I remember the drive well. It was winter, the car took a while to start, and smelt musty inside. So, I turned on the heater and opened the vents. When I picked up speed going down the Eastern Freeway, the leaves that had collected in the heating and vents blasted into the cabin in such numbers I felt like autumn had been revisited. It would eventually become my first car, much loved by me and my friends for its robust nature and inherent character. For me it was also a wonderful reminder of the many happy hours I spent driving Gran around the farm.

The priceless gift this experience left me with was to consider what I would think was important when I looked back on my life as an 80 year old.

Outward Bound

Gran Kent was not the only one to think that there might still be gold to be found on our farm. My other grandmother, Gran Shankly, even went as far as to give us a metal detector when I was in year 8 at school. We practiced using it by putting coins on the lawn and trying to locate them. Dad also got me to find metal pipes, where previously he was the only person who knew where they were. With the practice complete we then went down to the paddocks where the gold mining had been. Having walked around long enough to make Dad's dodgy ankle hurt, and only finding old tins and other scrap metal, Dad decided we should get in some expert help.

The expert was a neighbour who lived on the other side of what was Murray's farm. His house had no farmland, but Mr Flynn had been a boy when the gold mines on our farm were still operating prior to the first world war. He was also a bit of a fossicker himself, often sneaking onto our farm through a back gate. He had one of the last Valiant cars, the one with the giant boot, and we most often saw him near our tip, where he would remove parts of the old cars that had been dumped there. He would hide from us, and we would pretend not to see him.

Dad arranged for him to accompany me on a search for gold, with the spoils to be shared equally between us. I thought we would go to the big mine sites in the Cattle Yard paddock (where the tip was), or the 'Log Cabin' paddock (where the water hole was). But he said there was no point going there because the gold seams were deep down, and the Chinese had been through the mullock heaps and they left nothing behind. So, we went to the long string of individual mine shafts and mullock heaps in the 70 Acres.

I walked along in front and when the machine beeped, Mr Flynn would start digging. Again, we found a few stray bits of metal but not much else. In a couple of spots, we had dug down a foot or two, and even though the machine still beeped, Mr Flynn said there was no point in continuing. However, as we moved on, I noticed that he made a point of marking the ground nearby, so I figured he intended to return later and keep the spoils to himself. So, I had a change of plan. What Mr Flynn did not know was that the machine beeped when it hit the ground. So, my new plan was to subtly hit the ground every so often to give Mr Flynn a few extra places to dig on his return visit. I never found any gold, and if Mr Flynn did, he never told us.

I made a discovery that year, which occurred when I was staying on my friend Joe's farm. His sister also had some friends staying at the same time, and we were in the middle of a tennis game. The conversation had started on what age we had learnt to drive, and I mentioned that my father had also learnt to drive early because his father had only had one hand. (In the 1950s, possibly to help those wounded in wars, children were allowed to drive if accompanied by an adult with physical disabilities). This prompted a series of rapid-fire questions from Joe's mum that made focusing on the tennis difficult. Then she announced while a ball was in play that we were related.

It turned out that the stuffy old woman that I avoided by pretending to sleep was Gran Kent's sister. Joe and I were second cousins. Of course, this also extended to our sisters, although I did cause Joe's sister some amusement by introducing her on more than one occasion as my second cousin's sister. I also found out from Joe's mum that she and my Aunt Carolyn (Dad's sister) used to secretly meet up after the two sisters had a falling out. I later found out what the falling out was about.

When my Gran's father died, her sister's husband (Joe's Grandfather) was made the executor of the family trust, which at the time was quite substantial. However, after Gran's brother returned from the second world war, he got himself into considerable financial difficulty – I am not sure if it was gambling or bad business/investments – but it must have been big. The remaining family members were asked if they would help him out to save the family name. They were split 50/50. Gran and the doctor brother said no, her sister and the brother in trouble said yes. As the executor, the brother-in-law had the deciding vote – and voted with his wife. In that moment Gran lost all her inheritance. She also decided to never speak to her sister again. They both lived into their late 90s and for most of that time were less than five km from each other, but for those 40 plus years they never did see or speak to each other again. With this understanding, I never did introduce Joe to his Great Aunt.

Joe and I would remain good friends through school and beyond. He was a well-rounded and responsible individual with a strong work ethic, and we would often be in the same class. I think the school was hoping he would be a good influence on me. On the other hand, Michael and I were rarely put in the same class.

In year eight the only class Michael and I were in together was an elective – extra-maths. This was because we had both chosen to drop a language – he dropped Latin, I dropped French. Extra-maths was designed for kids that needed help with mathematics, as it was assumed that those who did not continue with a language needed assistance. The problem was that for at least half the extra-maths class this was a false assumption. It made life difficult for the young teacher, Mr Gray.

As usual, Michael was at the centre of the mayhem most of the time. He was sent to the corridor so often that Mr Gray had a desk placed there permanently. Sometimes he was even sent outside before the class had started. On one of these occasions, some chaos erupted in the class while Mr Gray was helping a struggling student with a maths problem, without looking up he sent Michael outside. Problem was, Michael was already in the corridor. Michael bounded back into the classroom to declare that this was proof that he had been victimised all along. This caused a great deal of amusement for everyone, including Mr Gray. But even after this, Michael still spent some part of nearly every class in the corridor. Mr Gray might have got it wrong once, but everyone, including Michael, knew that he was the troublemaker most of the time.

Michael also caused some trouble on school camp that year. It was the year that Outward Bound was introduced to the school. Outward Bound was an outdoor adventure program that escalated in difficulty each year and was designed to start in year 7 with a climax in year 10. Because the year's 7 and 9 camps were later in the year, we were the first group to attempt it. The school was not quite sure what we were in for, evident by the fact that we were all given a book of worksheets to complete from our class teachers. These were impossible to do around a campfire by torchlight, however the paper they were printed on did help us start the campfires.

Outward Bound was not your typical school camp. We never slept in the same place twice and we had to navigate our way from place to place carrying everything we were going to need with us and getting our water from the local streams. If we wanted to go to the toilet, we had to dig a hole. If we wanted to eat, we had to cook it. To spice things up a bit, we also did rock climbing, abseiling, rafting and white-water rapids on blow up lilos. By year 10 we were expected to do these things unsupervised.

In year 8, Michael and I were not only in the same group, but we were also in the same tent. Not that it was a tent. Outward Bound provided two plastic sheets and some long shoelace like ropes that we were required to build a shelter from. The thicker plastic sheet was to go on the ground, the clear plastic sheet was to go overhead. How effective the shelter was depended on us. The third person in our tent group was Gibbo.

The first night we had some guidance with the construction of our shelter, and it worked reasonably well. But as we progressed through the ten-day camp Michael became more inventive with the tent designs. The one I remember most had the ground sheet set on some squashed vegetation – an idea he sold to us as being like a mattress. At the same time the cover was tied exclusively to young saplings. The reason it was memorable was that it was a stormy night, and while all the other tents had a problem with water flooding down the hill, our layer of vegetation had kept us above the runoff. We might have been the only group not to get wet, except it was a windy night. The wind combined with the flexibility of the saplings to take our tent cover skyward like a kite, then plunge it back down onto our faces with a loud clap at either end of its journey. Gibbo was a plumber's son and was not impressed with Michael's inventiveness. So, Michael decided to play a trick on him.

The plot involved Michael taking advantage of the pre-dating technique of the day by telling Gibbo that a girl liked him, and telling the girl's friend to tell the girl that Gibbo liked her. He was expecting to be entertained by some clumsy courtship and then public embarrassment of Gibbo. What he did not consider was that they might like each other. Which was in fact what happened. Gibbo had a great camp, and we had more room to sleep.

This was not the only trick Michael attempted. He also told several kids that if they put their enamel bowls and cups upstream of some rapidly flowing water, they would be clean when they got them out at the bottom. Some of the dishes got lost along the way, so Michael had to donate his own dishes to those that had lost theirs. After which he shared my dishes, me eating first and Michael getting served after everyone else – which was often the burnt stuff at the bottom of the pot.

Like everything else in life, all of the Outward Bound challenges were easy for Michael. They were not so easy for other students, some of whom were pushed to their limits. I recall one girl being terrified of rock climbing. She froze halfway up the rock wall and cried for at least 10 minutes, then she let go of her handholds and clung to the safety rope. Unfortunately for her, she had climbed to one side of where the teacher was supporting the rope at the top, so when she let go she swung like a pendulum across the rock face, being bashed and bruised along the way. She eventually stopped swinging, but at this point the rope was found to be stuck. While the teachers tried to work out what to do, Michael casually climbed up the rock face like a giant spider, freeing the stuck rope along the way. He was initially thanked, then berated when they realised that he had done it all without safety equipment. He later abseiled down the face in three leaps when everyone else had taken at least a dozen. Walking with packs did not trouble him either, nor navigating by map and compass.

So, I was surprised at the end of the camp when everyone was asked to vote on who had handled the challenges the best, that I got the most votes. When a few were asked why they voted for me, the theme was that even though I was the smallest I had managed all the challenges and long hikes with a smile. But I credit the smile to

Michael as well. Perhaps that was the thing with Michael. You were either amused and impressed by him, or he drove you mad.

My other key memory of being introduced to Outward Bound was that none of us had showered for 10 days. We washed our hands and faces in cold water and Solvol (a harsh scrubbing soap), wore hats to hide our bad hair, and all looked as awful as each other. Because a lot of our spare clothes got wet early in the camp, most of us had worn the same clothes for days on end. Our parents complained about how bad we smelt, and my jeans could stand up on their own. We often got dirty and smelly on the farm, but apparently my parents thought this was much worse.

It was also in year 8 that we found a new way to get filthy on the farm. It started at another friend's place. Adds (pronounced Aids before we knew about AIDS) had older brothers and sisters and one of the things they did for fun was sit on an old car bonnet while it was towed behind a tractor tied to a long chain. You could feel every bump, but it was fun just trying to stay on. So, when Adds came to stay at our farm, we tried to reinvent it. We replaced the car bonnet with a sack stuffed with straw, and the chain with a hay twine. The hay twine broke on our first attempt, so we swapped it for a rope. We also used the Landcruiser instead of a tractor, so we were on our way to some seriously good fun. Because the Landcruiser could go faster, the trailing sack got the same sort of whipping motion as a water skier behind a boat. Also, because the sack was smaller, lighter and softer, we could get it airborne over bumps.

The only problem was the friction on the bottom of the sack would result in the bottom of the sack giving way, and the contents being suddenly ripped away. To minimise the friction, we generally tried to do this on wet grass. Sometimes, though, it was too wet, so on one occasion I covered Adds in mud from the spinning tyres. When summer came, the grass was drier and the ground harder, so the sacks hardly lasted any time at all. A new solution was required.

Because we were doing all of this without my parents' knowledge, we had to invent the solutions and source the materials ourselves. After several problematic versions we ended up with the ultimate towable device. It was an old truck tyre, into which we had placed two pieces of wood (to stop the riders falling through the hole), with a sack over the top (to stop the two pieces of wood pinching their backsides), attached by a rope that was attached through a hole drilled in the front and looped around the top (before the hole, the rope was around the tyre but the friction wore out the rope). The rope was about 20 metres long and looped onto the towbar via a spliced knot. It was more fun riding two at a time, and we always wore coveralls (full length overalls), even in summer. This kept the dirt off, most of which was cow dung. It also made falling off less painful – even though we often towed it at around 30 km/h – no one ever had more than a scrape or a bruise.

Just like in water skiing the driver of the vehicle had a key role to play. The fun was in the corners and the bumps, but also knowing the level of skill of the tyre riders. The less skilled had a slower ride, with gentle corners and tussocks for bumps. The experienced riders were given faster rides, wider corners and rougher bumps, often in combination. It was awesome fun, a favourite of most of our friends who visited the farm. When not in use the device itself was hidden in the trees in the 70 Acres. It is probably still there.

New Traditions

One of the reasons that we had a ready supply of coveralls was that they were what we wore when feeding out the hay and doing the cattle work – they dramatically reduced the amount of clothes that needed to be washed. This was a winter activity and Ballarat had a reputation for cold winters. To keep warm we often wore wool, but wool and hay are a bad combination. The hay seeds are designed to embed themselves in wool, and a woollen jumper or pair of socks full of hayseeds can take a long time to get them seed free. The solution was to wear gumboots over the socks, with the bottom of the coveralls over the outside of the boots. As we often had friends helping us, we had about a dozen sets of coveralls and gumboots in different sizes.

Mum also wore gumboots on Christmas day – which was in the middle of summer. This was because we had a tradition of having a game of cricket after the enormous Christmas lunch. Mum did not want to get hit in the shins with the ball, so she wore gumboots. This made it hard for her to run, and the rules were tippity-run – which means that if the bat hit the ball, you had to run. Despite the degree of difficulty, she would run as hard as she could from one end to the other – we all enjoyed it so much we did our best not to get her out.

It is interesting how traditions start. When we were little, in the old house, Christmas was unwrapping the presents in the morning, then getting dressed to visit our parents' families in Melbourne –

often without time to even play with our new toys. We would have lunch with Mum's side of the family, then cross town for dinner with Dad's side of the family. We then arrived home after dark too tired to even look at our presents.

Other than seeing all our cousins in a single day, the only other highlight was finding coins hidden in the plum pudding. They were genuine silver coins from prior to decimal currency and they were washed and reissued each year. If we found one and returned it, we were given actual money we could use. As I did not like plum pudding, finding the coins was the only reason to eat it. My cousin David took it to an extreme one year, eating serve after to serve to try and get as many coins as possible. I am not sure how much money he got, but I do remember he felt very ill afterwards. The fact the plum pudding was soaked in brandy may have had something to do with that.

It was a car accident that would put an end to this tradition. Fortunately, not a major one, but enough to destroy one of the car headlights and make us late for lunch. On arrival we were berated for being late and spoiling the turkey. I recall Mum calmly responding with, 'And Merry Christmas to you too'. There was a slight change in attitude after the reason for our late arrival was explained, but it was the last time we did the road trip for Christmas.

It took a couple of years in the new house to establish new traditions, the cricket game included. Our favourite part of the new tradition was Aunt Sal. She always wore red on Christmas day, had white hair and a big laugh, and to us she was even better than Santa Claus. She had a way of bringing out the fun in everyone, including Mum and Dad, and even when things did not go to plan, she would find a way for us to enjoy it. One year, Cindy gave me a small toy plastic twin-hulled sailboat. We took it and the two other sailboats I already owned (wooden yachts hand made by Aunt Sal's father – and given to me because he wanted them to be sailed not looked at). We took them down to the dam and set them up for a race. Sal provided the commentary which consisted of the new plastic sailing ship getting off to a great start, stretching its lead as it went up on one hull, and then slowing as it took on water, before sinking into the muddy water never to be seen again. Sal's commentary was so enthusiastic and engaging that the loss of the new toy seemed a small price to pay for the joy she brought to the experience.

I think it was the Christmas after Deb's operation that we all really appreciated how fortunate we were to be together for Christmas. But it took another couple of years to feel like it was a tradition.

We did not really have many other traditions. Each year seemed to bring its own version – some feasts, some famines. We also shared our house with different people along the way. Not only relatives and friends, but we also hosted foreign workers as part of the International Future Farmers program. As the name suggests it was an exchange program for individuals who were planning to run a farm at some point in their future. The idea was that they would experience other ways of farming before taking on the farm they grew up on, so that they would become better farmers themselves.

The first was an American whose stay started in January and coincided with a locust plague. He had blonde hair and fair skin, which he claimed tanned easily, but he was badly sunburnt on his first day. He was also from the Rocky Mountains and had never seen the beach. When we took him to the beach, it was the first time he had worn bare feet outdoors. He yelled as only an American can as he tried to walk and run across the hot dry sand to the water. That was one of the benefits of having a future farmer stay with us, we went on more trips to show them things.

The locusts ate everything. There was no grass left in the paddocks, and while driving through the fields in summer usually raised a dust cloud behind the vehicle, thanks to the locusts, it also raised a similar cloud in front of the vehicle – hundreds of the insects lifting off the ground. Riding our bikes would also raise a similar cloud, which we would the ride into. We used to joke about it feeling like we were being shot at as the locusts bounced off our faces, bodies, and limbs.

The second future farmer was a female. She was very good natured, but not very fit, and as part of the deal was that they worked on the farm this caused a few challenges. As kids we preferred her company and she seemed to enjoy ours. Given that the motivation for participating in the program was Mum's belief that, because she could not afford to take us to the world, she would get others to bring the world to us – our second guest did a much better job than the first.

The third was a Kiwi from the southern end of the North Island of New Zealand. I don't recall how long he stayed but Jim did purchase a car and drove himself places at various times. He had a good sense of humour and seemed as happy in our company as in our parents'. I don't recall how old I was when he was there, possibly year 8, because when he wanted to go camping, I suggested we go to the Grampians – which was where we had been for Outward Bound.

Perhaps the thing that made Jim more memorable was that when I was older, he would write to Dad to express his gratitude for his time on our farm and inform us that he was now running his family farm, and invited me to go and work with him. It was an invitation I enthusiastically accepted, and an experience from which I learnt a lot.

Back on the farm, we had a bumper year for haymaking. We normally made about 6,000 to 7,000 bales – in this year we made more than double that. In part it was because other farms also had bumper years and having filled their haysheds, they offered some of their paddocks to us to cut and bale. I am not sure of the finances, but I do remember it was a long summer on the tractor, and it was also the only time we baled an oat crop.

We had two permanent haysheds, each stored 3,000 bales. In a good year we also created a temporary haystack of around 1,000 bales that we had to put a temporary roof on. In the bumper year we had another four haystacks of 2,000 bales each. These were then topped with sheets of corrugated iron weighted down by hay bales. Most of this hay would be sold over several years – trucked to farmers many hours away who were in drought conditions. Before this we would have a mouse plague – Mum blamed it on the oat hay, and the mice certainly liked that the most. But given our neighbours and nearby districts also had a mice plague I think it was a broader issue.

While all these events are hard to place in time, my school years are a little easier, and year 9 was the most memorable.

Year 9

Year 9 did not start out well. There was a new girl at school, Lisa. She was Italian and shorter than me, which was a bonus. She also had curves in all the right places and a pretty face – she was also aware of her assets. Within two days of starting school, she decided to sit next to me on the bus – an arrangement that would continue for the rest of our school days. We would always be mates, never boyfriend and girlfriend. In many ways she was a female version of Michael, except only half his size – and she never got caught.

Her first piece of mischief was in maths class on Valentine's Day – we had talked about how stupid the messages in the cards were on the way in. Then she wrote me one. It read, 'My love for you is so great I want to f_ck you in a crate'. I chuckled, others wanted to see it, and so it got passed around the class. Then the maths teacher spotted it, and the unfortunate boy who was holding it was sent to the headmaster. I took one look at her mask of innocence and knew that she was trouble.

The maths teacher was not an emotionally stable man. When angry he liked to squeeze a student's earlobe between his thumbnail and a fingernail. It was very painful. I found this out firsthand one morning when I tried to explain to him that I was in fact early when he was telling me off for being late. This was because the bus usually caused us to arrive 10 minutes late to the first class. This fact was known and accepted by all the teachers. On this morning, we had missed the bus, so Mum had driven us all the way to school, which was much faster, and so we were only five minutes late to class. I was sent to the headmaster for being cheeky.

It was a blessing. I was transferred from his class into Mr Leather's maths class – which was meant to be some sort of downgrade – however he was a much better teacher, and the class was much more fun. Part of the fun was that he was so passionate about explaining the maths that on one occasion when he could not find the duster, he wiped the chalk off the blackboard with his tie. From that moment on we would try and get to the classroom first so we could hide the dusters from him. After wiping the board with his coat sleeves, paper, and anything else he could find, he eventually opted to carry a duster with him. Not that it curbed his enthusiasm. On one occasion he turned to draw a line on the board with such gusto he put the end of the metre ruler through the board.

That the class was more mischievous should not have been that surprising. From year 9 on, the school arranged to have the maths and English classes for the year level taught at the same time and allocated the students into four classes based on their grades in the subject. The best students were in class A, and the worst in class D. After my move to Mr Leather's class, I was now in class B for both maths and English. Where class A had students that were capable and worked hard, class B had a mixture of those who were less capable and worked hard, and those that were capable but did not work. This latter cohort were the troublemakers, and chief amongst them in both classes was Michael.

Year 9 English was the most memorable of all my classes. Mrs B was our teacher, and like Mr Leather she was passionate about the subject and keen to see us reach our potential. She was also willing to attempt the unconventional to try and get the best out of us. It did not always work, particularly with both Lisa and Michael in the class.

Our regular classroom for English had the chairs with a table built in that could be readily rearranged around the room. The only problem was that we had four left-handed students and only three left-handed desks. So, there was always a scramble at the start of the class to get to the desks, which were nearly always in different places to the last time. Having found the desk, the next scramble was to try and move it as close to the heating as possible, because this was Ballarat, and the classrooms were cold. This meant that every class started in a state of chaos, so that Mrs B had to regularly exert a level of crowd control. This she did in a way that was both good humoured as well as leaving us in no doubt that she was in control. There were however three instances when the mayhem got the better of her.

The first of these was early in the year when we had to give a two-minute oral presentation to the class on a topic of our own choosing. Normally, the order of delivery was known, but she had said we all had to be ready to go first and she would decide on the day whose turn it was. A group of us had been acting up, and so not surprisingly she decided it was our turn to present. Lisa went first and delivered a polished presentation, with props, on the seal fur trade. She got full marks. I was up next, I had not prepared anything, so I said my topic was on beef farming and gave a run-through of the year on a beef farm. I also got full marks. A new kid Dave was up next, he was also unprepared, but inspired by my efforts he decided to give a run-through of a year on a sheep farm. He got zero marks. At this point the class got rowdy, although largely impressed by Mrs B's willingness to mark things as she saw them. Next up was Michael, he was also unprepared, but recognising that originality appeared to be appreciated he decided to give a run through of the history of his accidents.

This started off calmly with some early childhood instances and pointing to various scars on his body. Then he started doing re-enactments of some of the accidents. This included being hit on the head by a slide in grade one, which he demonstrated by grabbing a nearby textbook and hitting himself on the head and falling to the ground, at which point the textbook was raised into the air only to descend again just as he rolled his head away. He also demonstrated how he broke his arm while riding a bike down a hill at high speed with his feet on the handlebars – this part of the presentation included him using one of the desks as a prop. He showed us how he was peddling hard to catch up to his friends on faster bikes, only to have the pedals going so fast he had to get his feet out of the way, which he did by putting them on the handlebars, (the top of the desk), only to have it hit a bump and throw him violently onto the side of the road – at this point Michael flung himself and the desk into a tumbling roll across the room. He then sprung up and rolled up his shirt sleeve to show us the scar from the stitches as proof of the validity of his description of events. He also covered how his father had accidently put a nail through some of his son's fingers with an illegally modified nail gun, as well as a few sports injuries. All of this was described in detail while being re-enacted with high energy and a complete disregard for his own safety as he portrayed each violent episode. It was one of the funniest presentations I have ever see – the entire class and Mrs B were laughing. It went well over time, but no one cared, and at the end of it all, Michael got zero marks for his presentation. This launched him into a strenuous debate on the merits of the marking system, which created even more amusement with Mrs B and the class but left his grade unchanged.

That was the thing with Mrs B, she was open to interaction with the class, particularly if it was entertaining, but she usually had the final say. The second incident that caused a bit of mayhem had its origins with what the school fed the boarders. Put simply, it was too many beans. We had several boarders in the class including Dave, he was sitting next to Michael, and Michael was complaining loudly about Dave's farts. Not surprisingly Mrs B was having none of it. Michael then started moving his desk across the room to be further away, and was sent back, but not without making a commotion about it, even opening the window despite the cold outside. Then Dave let one rip, and Michael yelled and jumped out the window. The class burst into laughter as Mrs B started yelling at Michael to get back in the classroom or be sent to the headmaster. Then the smell hit her and us, and everyone including Dave ran for the nearest door or window to get away from it. After the air had cleared, Mrs B got us all back into the room and told everyone that if they needed to fart then they had to leave the room first. The rest of the class was peppered with fake fart noises, and worried looks, but no further smells. Although Dave did step outside a couple of times.

The third incident happened later in the year. We were studying the play *The Big Men Fly* and Mrs B thought that we would learn it better if we acted it out. She was then impressed enough with how we portrayed it to decide to put it on as a play for our parents. For this she managed to get access to a relatively unused classroom in the old junior school, and those of us who had main parts were required to do practice after school. This included Michael, Lisa and Dave.

On one occasion Michael had gone home and was followed back to school by his dog Tarzan, who stood outside and howled every time Michael spoke, which was often as he had a main role. This really got on Mrs B's nerves. Michael pretended not to know who owned the dog.

I don't recall all of the roles, but I do know that I had the role of the recruiting agent, Michael was the Big Man, and Lisa and Dave were the TV commentators. The set was arranged with blackout curtains so that we could have lights out between changes in sets. Michael was dressed as a footballer, while the rest of us wore suits. While I had some leniency in my appearance, Lisa and Dave were meant to be well groomed. As we got closer to opening night, Mrs B was getting a bit of pre-show anxiety. She was particularly frustrated by the fact that despite her various efforts backstage, Dave would arrive on stage looking a bit dishevelled. She would draw attention to the fact that Lisa managed to always look the part and could not understand how no amount of hairspray could keep his hair in place.

Lisa would join in on the discussions sharing Mrs B's puzzlement that Dave was so incapable of keeping himself well-groomed for the duration of the play. When Dave was told off by Mrs B, Lisa would refute Dave's attempts at saying that it was not his fault and point out that Lisa was on and off the stage the same amount of time he was. At the final practice Mrs B got the lighting kids to put the lights on early between the set changes and found Michael and David wrestling on the ground. At this point Mrs B stepped forward, shouting something about knowing it was Michael the whole time, and then started kicking him while he was still entangled with Dave. She did not stop until Michael was standing up, and even then, she continued to yell at him for a bit.

Michael and Lisa had been messing with Dave's appearance the whole time. Lisa started it by making little changes to Dave's clothes while he wasn't looking. Then Michael took over and ruffled his hair and pulled at his clothes. So, Dave had no choice but to try and defend himself physically during the set changes. Fortunately, he was built like a bullock, and was athletic enough to be the only other year 9 boy besides Michael to be in the senior football team. Subsequently, the tussles between sets got more rigorous as we got closer to opening night, until the lights came on with the two of them grappling on the ground.

That was the last time Michael messed with Dave between sets, and the play was well received by the audience. We all knew Mrs B should not have kicked Michael, but none of us wanted her to get in trouble for it. Everyone, including Michael, understood that she had put up with a lot that year, was a good person, and everyone has a breaking point – particularly when Michael is involved.

The week after the play finished, we were off to the Otway Ranges for Outward Bound, and Michael would get under Mr Leather's skin enough for him to yell at Michael that he was the sort of person that kills people in the bush. I was not in Michael's group, but I heard that the reason for this outburst was that Michael had been allocated the role of 'tail-end Charlie', who was meant to alert the group if anyone fell behind them, but he was found walking near the front of the group. Fortunately, no one in their group was hurt or missing, which could not be said for the group I was with.

The Otway Ranges is a rainforest, and in the late spring of 1980 it rained a lot. The persistent rain not only dampened the forest and our clothes, but it also dampened our spirits, particularly when we were told that our group would not be doing the white-water rafting as the volume of rain had made it unsafe. It was shortly after this that we reached one of the base camps for the night and one of the boys in the group intentionally mispronounced a girl's surname to call her 'stinkers'. I doubt that she smelt any worse than the rest of us, but it distressed her enough for her to leave the group.

Unfortunately, her departure was not realised until close to dusk, at which point repeated head counts and a check to see if she had gone to the toilet confirmed that we were one person short. Given that the camp was next to a flowing river, there was genuine concern for her safety. The male teacher with the group along with two of the larger boys then embarked on a search down river, equipped with a long rope and bright torches. After some time, they returned to camp soaking wet and empty handed.

In the meantime, the rest of us had formed a search line and spread inland and upstream, but we were also unsuccessful. The teachers and camp coordinators were now clearly distressed but trying to hide it. They were also trying to decide what to do with the rest of us. Belatedly, they realised that the searching meant that many people had not been able to set up our tents, and so we were all told to relocate our belongings into the basecamp tent where we would sleep for the night.

The male teacher and two boys then left to search upstream while we got the fire going and started preparing the meal. At some point during all of this, the teachers had also used the emergency radio to call for help. That help arrived about five minutes after the missing girl walked back into the campsite and about 20 minutes before the male teacher and the two boys returned.

It turned out she had gone just far enough away to get some privacy and had hidden from our search party because she had mistaken the two boys she saw as people looking for firewood. The extra help departed, and we all tried to pretend that everything was back to normal. But it wasn't – one of the boys who had been searching up and down the river with the teacher got hypothermia.

The Outward Bound coordinator devised a plan. We had to find the driest sleeping bag (most of them were at least partially wet), then he and another boy would share the sleeping bag in their underwear, while the rest of us created a mass of warm bodies around them in our own sleeping bags. It worked. Within a couple of hours he was warm enough for the body oven we had created to be disbanded. But there was more drama to come. Later in the night one of the main poles holding up the giant tent (there were over 20 of us with space to spare) fell down. Some of us got up and tried to fix it, but the problem was that the ground was so wet that the tent pegs just slipped straight out. So, we just gave up on it and all slept under the collapsed tent.

Fortunately, the rain stopped, and we had good weather for the remainder of the camp. I also won some money on a bet, for doing forty push-ups with a full backpack on. My tent partner was not so fortunate. Early in the camp a leech attached itself to his eyelid while he slept. When he pulled it off as he woke, it caused his eye to inflame, and it remained that way for the remainder of the camp. The rest of us also got bitten by leeches, but no one else got one on their eye. Outward Bound was intended to test and strengthen our resilience with each year being more challenging – after this experience lots of students were concerned about how tough the year 10 camp was going to be. I was looking forward to it. I had faced tougher challenges earlier in the year – when Deb was told her brain tumour had relapsed.

Milking Cows in the Night

It was in the middle of her year 12 (my year 9) that Deb went for her third anniversary check-up expecting the same all clear she had received the previous two times. She was devastated to find that there had been some regrowth, and she would need to have another operation, not only because it would prevent her from finishing school with her friends, but also because it tilted the odds of a permanent recovery against her. Having lost her buddy from her first time in hospital to cancer already, she was all too aware how important beating the odds were.

The other thing that was different this time around was that she knew how hard the path to recovery was likely to be. Although, because it is brain surgery, in some ways she didn't. Deb ended up having another brain operation when she was in her early 30s. With each of the three operations she lost something different and had to retrain her brain to try and get it back. Some things never came back.

Watching Deb try to relearn things that we do without thinking was tough, but nothing compared to the challenge she had. Needing to relearn how to swallow when you are born knowing it is particularly hard, and failed attempts were very embarrassing for her. Because of this, Deb avoided eating in public for 18 months after one of her operations as she tried to relearn this inherent skill.

For the rest of the family, the second time around was a lot more organised. We had family friends, Mac and Felty, come and stay on the farm along with their pre-school aged children. This enabled both my parents to be with Deb in the first few intense weeks. It also meant that for Barb, Cindy, and I, the daily routine was much the same. The one big difference for me was that I had to milk Deb's two cows twice a day.

As a rule, cows are accustomed to being milked at dawn and dusk. The problem I had was that I took a lot longer to milk them than Deb did, and so I needed to start earlier to fit the chore in before going to school. Given that it was mid-winter when the nights are long and the days are short, that required me starting in the dark. The cows were not happy about this arrangement and given that they had 18 acres to hide from me in, I also had to start even earlier to allow time for finding them and getting them into the sheep yards next to the shearing shed, which was where the milking was done.

I think I had to do the milking for about 10 weeks, and I did not mind it toward the end. The days were longer, and the cows came to the yards to be milked instead of hiding from me hoping that Deb would show up. I even got better at milking. But as soon as Deb said she would like to milk again, I was delighted to give it back.

This was not the only chore I did at night. From an early age I had a steady hand, so when Dad was fixing something late at night and needed an extra pair of hands, he would wake me up. Acting as a human clamp for various things I got a close-up view on how to solder electrical wires, splice rope, and repair various pieces of equipment. The only one I didn't like was the soldering. I was often required to hold small pieces of wire very close to a large, very hot, soldering iron and Dad's hands were not as steady as mine.

Getting up before dawn was not unusual for me. I was often first up to get through the bathroom before my sisters, and in winter to have time to heat the milk on the stove – we did not have a microwave. My alarm clock had been owned by my grandfather. It was a beautiful art deco device that combined an alarm clock with a kettle and teapot. The kettle was set to boil just before the alarm went off and was structured in such a way that the boiling water was automatically transferred into the teapot – so that a warm cup of tea greeted the person as they woke. There were only two problems, one was that I did not drink tea, and the other was that anytime it was turned off and on again, the clock would change direction. Which was why one night dad found me showered, dressed and getting breakfast ready at three in the morning.

Dad was often up late. He, like other farmers, also had lots of bumps and scrapes. On one occasion he had some serious bruising under his thumbnail. The doctor offered to cut a hole in it for him, or suggested that Dad could try drilling a hole himself, as he would be able to know when to stop drilling. Dad decided that drinking some brandy to dull the pain would be a good idea before he started. Numerous brandies later, he realised that having a steady hand was more important when trying to use a large drill to put a small hole in your own thumbnail. Fortunately, he aborted the mission before he did too much damage to himself.

Mum had worries of her own. Her main concerns were for Deb. Knowing that Deb was at high risk of more cancer after her first operation, Mum had enrolled in a librarianship degree at the local university to help keep her mind occupied. Now with more to worry about after the second operation, she enrolled in a master's degree, and would eventually become a lecturer. In doing so, she introduced computing to the house. This was initially on paper cards. Each instruction had to be marked on a series of cards, and the cards fed into the computer in the right order for the code to run. It was a very painful way to work, and Mum was extremely protective of her boxes of cards.

It would not be until the end of year 10 that we got our first computer. It had 16 kilobytes of internal memory, a cassette tape recorder as the storage device, and an old portable black and white TV for the screen. It may not sound like much, but it was a massive leap forward from the card systems of a year earlier. It would also change my career choices.

For her part Deb was keen on getting on with life. She had been told that she was unlikely to live to 30, and so she set her sights on living life to the fullest before then. For Deb, this was not about partying hard and travelling to exotic destinations. To Deb, alcohol was a reminder of a faulty brain, and she had been close enough to death to know what was important to her. So, she accelerated towards being an adult.

I was still very much a kid, and so to me this felt like she was moving away, not physically but emotionally. I did my best to bring her back to childhood and she never resisted. It was not like she was wanting to leave her childhood; she just knew she had a lot she wanted to do in her life and not much time to do it in.

Lessons in Management

By the start of year 10 my voice had broken so that now my voice was indistinguishable from Dad's. The timing is relatively easy to place as at the start of year 9 I coxed a rowing crew, the fifth crew, and my voice would jump between octaves in the middle of instructions – much to the amusement of the crew. They were all at least two years older than me and as our coach was not part of the school and did not arrive at training until he had finished work, we often started training by taking the boat to less used parts of the lake where some of the crew would smoke a cigarette, before rowing over to where we had agreed to meet the coach.

Despite this unconventional training program, we won our division at the annual 'Head of the Lake' competition that year. In the lead up to that we also won our division in a regatta on the lake, which including beating the fourth crew in the final. The regatta was held on a very windy day, so much so that all of the 1,000 metre events were held over the first half of the course so that the boats could be held at the start. This meant that we finished the race in the middle of the lake, and not realising we needed to go to the normal finish line to collect the trophy, we rowed back to the sheds without it.

Apparently, it was my coxing performance in this race that put me in the frame to be the cox of the first crew the following year. Dad was with the head coach on the shore behind the starting line and as they watched the race unfold, the head coach apparently remarked on the fact that ours was the only boat going in a straight line.   The try-outs for the various senior crews were done during the pre-season rowing camp during the last two weeks of the summer holidays. This involved eight straight days of rowing, with 20 rowers and five coxes being shuffled into different boats as the coaches tried to settle on the composition of the crews.

The school had won the last four Head of the Lake competitions, and given St Pat's always won the football, rowing had an elevated sense of importance within the school. It also required a lot of commitment from those involved, training four nights a week and all day Saturday – unless there was a rowing competition. It seemed like every second week, the crews would need to either be up early Saturday, or on a few occasions travel on Friday and stay overnight for the competition the following day.

Toward the end of the rowing camp, it was apparent that the coaches had settled on two crews – a lightweight crew, most of whom had rowed together as the thirds the year before, and a heavier weight crew drawn from multiple crews the year before. The coxing was also down to two people – the headmaster's son (who had arrived at the school with his father the year before) and me. I assumed he would get it as he had coxed a year longer than me, and he was the headmaster's son.

There was a major sailing regatta on the penultimate day of the rowing camp so the coaches were shore bound and we were required to row back and forth close to the shore so they could watch on and give instructions. We had been doing this for a while without incident, when I noticed that the other crew was heading directly toward us, I called my crew to a halt and got them all to yell at the other crew to stop. By the time the other crew paid attention it was too late, the bows of the two boats collided, with the front of our boat punching a hole in the front of theirs. I don't recall how the punctured boat was returned to the shed, but the next day the lightweight crew was told they were the first crew, and I was told that I was their cox. So began my first experience of management.

The previous year I had simply steered the boat. But the head coach set the bar higher, he wanted me to be his eyes and ears and he gave me licence to change the tempo during races. He insisted that a good cox could make the boat go faster and implied that the regatta race that my crew had won the year before was due in part to me.

Our first competitive race was on the Yarra during the Moomba festival, the day after AC/DC played at the Myer Music Bowl. We had arrived the night before in a school bus with the rowing boats in tow but were unable to get access to the rowing sheds due to the concert crowd. Conscious that valuable and fragile rowing boats and a rough rock and roll crowd were probably not a good mix, the teachers diverted to Melbourne Grammar and unloaded the boats there for the night, before returning to the boat sheds alongside the Yarra for us to unpack our sleeping bags and find a space on the wooden floor for the night.

Later some of the rowers decided to go and take a look at the concert and so I joined them and while we could not see a lot, the noise and energy from the concert was powerful. The next day we tried to harness some of that energy into our race. Because most of the crew were the same as the thirds from the previous year, we had to race in a different class against adult rowers in the same weight division. I also had to be weighed, but like a jockey, I had to weigh in at a minimum weight, in this case 50 kg. I only weighed 40 kg, so I had to carry around 10 kg of bolts in a padded bag.

It was my first race on a curved course. The race started upstream of Punt Road, and as we were on the north side, we had the inside running of the bend ahead of the Swan Street bridge. There was a race marshal at the bend, and he was yelling at me to stay within my lane or be disqualified. I realised I needed to get around a buoy and tried hard to turn the boat without unbalancing the crew. I achieved it, just, the buoy went under the rigging between the boat and the oars. We won that race, putting us into the final, but we came second in the final when we stayed in the middle of the lane. For the rest of the season, we would be beaten by the same crew in every competition by a very small margin.

While trimming the corner in the first race was accidental, two other incidents gave me confidence in the responsibility of managing the team. The first occurred on a Saturday when we shared the lake with yachts – we were on the rowing course and the yachts were sailing across them. The yachts had right of way. I noticed that there was only a small gap in the constant flow of yachts across our path, and while the coach was in mid-instruction to one of the crew about his technique, I ordered the crew up to full speed to ensure they got through the gap. They responded immediately, we got through, the coaches had to wait, and when they re-joined us, the coach complimented me on my initiative. More importantly, I realised that good decisions and direction are valued and respected, particularly by those receiving the directions.

The second instance occurred later in the season. The improvement of the crew had stalled, and I was noticing that one of the rowers was often out of time, and his technique was sloppy. I quietly alerted the coach, he realised I was right and when we could not fix it, he decided to change the crew. This was obviously an unhappy event for the crew member who left, but the rest of the crew were pleased, particularly as we now went faster. So, I realised that being nice to one team member can result in doing the wrong thing to everyone else, which was another valuable lesson in management. I had also earnt the respect of the crew, which provided another lesson – respect is more important than popularity. Popularity can be fleeting, but people inevitably like those they respect in the long term.

Back on the farm I was also getting lessons in management, helped by the fact that I had the same voice as Dad. It was Dad's first year as the captain of the Haddon Fire Brigade, which was how long the local brigade had existed. As I was only 15, I was not eligible to be a member of the brigade, but as with a lot of other things Dad did, I was there anyway. I was also only eligible to drive the tractor on the road if it was going from one part of our property to another, but with the tractor towing a trailer with a full fire tank and crew, the local police stopped traffic to wave me through on the way to a fire.

Another incident involving the police occurred at Easter. The first three boys crews and the first two girls crews were in Mildura for the Easter rowing competition. We had all been to a dinner hosted by one of the rower's families – he was one of many boarders who came from Mildura. After we had returned to our accommodation, about a dozen of us decided to go for a walk to have a look around the town, including the headmaster's son. Some of the older boys were carrying beers despite being underage. So, when a police car pulled us over with the sirens on, we thought they were going to be in trouble. After a brief exchange the police put us into the back of the divvy van. I can remember two things from the short ride – the worried looks and an empty stubby rolling across the floor as the car accelerated and braked or turned corners. The van returned us to our accommodation and sent one of us to get a teacher. They had an exchange out of earshot, and we were sent to our rooms. We found out the next day that there was also a hot-rod car convention on in Mildura which had got out of hand, so the police had applied a local curfew. We had been inadvertently walking toward the chaos, the police had picked us up and taken us home for our safety. It is this sort of pragmatism that was commonplace in country Australia during my childhood. But what I have discovered over the years is that good management is far too rare.

Perhaps that was why Dad was put in charge of just about everything in the district – he was known and respected as a good manager of people. Although even he learnt things along the way. One of these lessons occurred in his first year as Captain, and I had the good fortune to learn it with him. It occurred when we had our first wild-fire under his command. Fortunately, it was on farmland not in the bushland. It was also before the brigade had a fire truck of its own.

Dad and I arrived at the fire at the same time as a fire truck from the next brigade. Seeing that the truck had a driver but no crew, we got onto the truck, started the pumps, and headed into the fire. The driver was an experienced firefighter, and the vice-captain of the other brigade, so he knew what he was doing. The fire was heading south, blown by a north wind, but a westerly wind change was expected, so he drove onto the burnt ground behind the fire, and we started putting out the east flank. In the process we became completely engulfed by smoke, being able to see less than 30 metres in any direction.

While we were doing this, other trucks were on their way from other brigades and the district fire controller was calling out over the radio asking to speak to the Haddon captain. When he found out that Dad was on a truck in the middle of the fire, he ripped into him, instructed him to get out of there as quickly as possible and find a position where he could see what was going on. And that in the meantime he was going to assume the worst and send everything. When we got out of the fire and up onto a hill Dad was still a bit shaken by the dressing down, so he told me what to say and I radioed in the instructions. It was not a major fire, and most of the trucks were sent home before they arrived, but it was an important lesson in management. The most important part of the job is to make the right decisions and articulate them clearly – and you can't do that if you are fighting fires yourself.

One of the reasons Dad was such a good manager was his humour and humility. He never sought status, nor wielded power unjustly. He genuinely endeavoured to do the right thing, even if that meant bending or breaking the rules. Because of this people loved working with him and politics evaporated around him. Like the rest of my childhood, I thought this was normal, but unfortunately, I have since discovered good managers are far too rare. I think this is because it is not taught – I have had the good fortune to be mentored and to mentor others in management and from this I know that it is a transferable skill. I had the good fortune of observing and absorbing it as part of my childhood.

Year 10

At the start of year 10, the school introduced an extra layer of management. This included a female vice-principal, and a school marshal. The vice-principal had two children – a boy in my year, and a girl in Barb's year. The boy was known as Moose and was large and loud and would become good friends with Michael and me. The marshal was an ex-army officer, and his primary role was to deal with discipline so that from year 10 onward we would be sent to the marshal instead of the headmaster.

My first encounter with the marshal was a result of a prank played on me by Michael and Moose. The school had a box for lost property which was referred to as the pound box. It was about 1.5 metres long, 50 cm tall and 75 cm wide. One lunchtime, we were walking past it when Moose noticed that it was unlocked. Opening it up revealed a largely empty box with a motley collection of smelly clothes and shoes. A little disappointed in this, the two of them decided it would be good to see if I could fit in the box. They promised not to lock me in, but that did not stop them from doing just that – then the bell went for the start of class, and they departed.

Not happy about the arrangement I called out a few times but got no response. So, I decided to take matters into my own hands and kicked out the end of the box. As I was crawling out of the box a teacher came past and told me off for damaging school property. When I started to defend my actions, she said that I could explain it to the marshal and walked me to his office. I had to wait outside for a few minutes while she spoke to him, then she left giving me a look of vindication and victory. So, I entered his office a little nervously. Before I even had a chance to sit down, he said "Michael and Moose put you in there?" My face must have betrayed my thoughts, as I was thinking "How did you know?" Then he simply said, "tell those two not to do it again to you or anyone else", then waved for me to leave the room.

Pranks were common and often physical. They were also more readily done on your friends than others. But everyone was fair game. In Commerce we were doing an exercise on price monitoring where we were sent out in threes to visit the same store and record the prices of a set of products every week – like a miniature version of the Consumer Price Index. I was in the same group as Lisa and Slug, and the store we were monitoring was the supermarket near the school, which also happened to be where my sister Deb now worked.

After our first visit to the store Lisa handed Slug and I a chocolate bar each on the way back to school. I had stopped to talk to Deb and so I assumed she had paid for it, particularly because she always had money. When she said that she hadn't paid I was worried it would get Deb into trouble. This amused Lisa and Slug and so almost every time we visited the store, they would produce something from their pockets on the way back to school just to get a rise out of me. I never actually saw them take anything, and they both could afford to buy it, so to this day I don't know if they were just pranking me or stealing – but they certainly enjoyed provoking me about it.

Michael enjoyed provoking Moose, in part because Moose was incapable of subtlety. They both had a similar sense of humour and high pain threshold and so even if the other person was hurt, they would both laugh about it. Moving out of the way of a fist so that it hit a wall was a common event between the two of them, although Michael seemed to fair better. Others also got caught up in the antics, often to their detriment.

Chalk and duster fights had been reasonably common for my entire schooling life, perhaps inspired by teachers who would throw chalk at students to get their attention. If we were in an empty classroom unsupervised it would not take long for these instruments of learning to be repurposed as throwing weapons. Being hit with the duster hurt less, but it left an obvious mark. Being hit with chalk could be painful, particularly as we got older. On one occasion I deflected a piece of chalk heading for my head with my forearm. It hit my watch face and shattered it. Watches were treasured, so this was a big deal. Interestingly, the thought that the chalk was thrown too hard did not occur to any of us.

A common prank for when we were standing around talking, was for someone to crouch down on their hands and knees behind someone in a conversation and have the person they were talking to push them so that they fell over the top of the person crouching. It became so common it would happen to multiple people a day. It had happened to me a few times before Moose overdid it. I was talking to him with books in hand before a class when one of the boarders crouched down behind me, Moose stepped forward and shoved me hard, so that I got airborne. I landed on my head, knocked unconscious. The floor was a thin layer of carpet squares on concrete, and other kids said they heard my spine crack like a series of knuckles when I landed. I don't recall it at all. I do remember coming to and vomiting in a nearby bin, before one of my more responsible friends, probably Joe, took me to the sick bay. From there Mum took me to hospital, where I remember the nurses wanting to keep me awake while all I wanted to do was sleep.

When I got back to school the following week no one was doing the crouching prank. Many years and four more concussions (three playing football, one from a car accident) later I suffer from frequent migraines. The doctors have told me that concussions are cumulative, once you have had one you are more vulnerable to others, and that increases with every occurrence, and the migraines are most likely a result of the concussions.

Moose also managed to concuss a classmate that year with a loose elbow while dancing. The unfortunate recipient was Ben, from the rice farm. It would be Ben's last year at the school. But concussion aside, the physical pranks were generally easier to handle than the non-physical ones. I think one of the benefits of co-ed schools is that girls get a haven from other girls when things turn against them. For my entire life I have had sisters and female friends, and I have watched in bafflement as they share too much with each other, and then turn that information against each other. It is in these times when the simpler, less sensitive, male friendships can at least provide some continuity and a different perspective. This is not to say that male friendships are better – males can be equally cruel.

In this prank ridden landscape, it was not always easy for us to spot bullying. I am ashamed to admit that I unwittingly contributed to a boy's misery. After a physical education class, it was noticed that one of the athletic boys had not participated because he was injured. When we returned to the change rooms, another boy, Trevor (not his actual name), who was a nice person and an excellent musician, but who was not athletic and prone to perspiration, was changing back into his school uniform when he realised that someone had drawn on his shirt. It was a temperature gauge in his armpit. I was one of the many kids who laughed. That was Trevor's last day at the school, he felt so hurt and unwelcome he could not come back. The boy who did the writing was expelled.

By year 10, boys and girls were separated for physical education, except for dance classes. We were forced to dance with partners not of our choosing. The boys looked forward to the dance sessions, the girls loathed them. The dances were old-fashioned square dancing and waltzing – which required proximity between the dance partners. The difference in attitude was more down to glass-half-full and glass-half-empty, possibly with some probability thrown in. The boys were glass-half-full, thinking about the opportunity of dancing with some of the girls they liked, ignoring the probability of dancing with girls they did not care for. The girls were glass-half-empty, dreading dancing with the boys they disliked, and ignoring the possibility of dancing with the boys they liked.

Year 10 was also the pinnacle of Outward Bound, and the attitude toward it was similarly divided between the boys and girls. The groups themselves would be much smaller, and not co-ed. We were expected to be able to self-navigate and hike our way across the Grampians over several days before forming larger groups and rafting across a lake.

As part of our preparation for the camp we were to pick our own group, which was to consist of 12 boys or girls, four tents of three people. Michael and I were in the same group, and so I expected it to be an eventful camp, particularly after the previous years' experience. Of the remaining 10 in our group, most were from farms. It certainly started out differently, after arriving together and being given our allocation of food and equipment, the groups of 12 were then dropped off at different points throughout the Grampians with a map that had our current location and a series of checkpoints that we were to navigate our way to over the next seven days. We were apparently unsupervised, although we found out later that we were being followed from a distance the whole time.

Because we were all reasonably athletic and accustomed to the outdoors, we made it to each checkpoint with time to spare and then set off to see if we could find any of the other groups. On the fourth night we found one of the girls groups. They were finding it tougher going than us and were way behind on their checkpoints.

We also worked out that we were meant to end up in the same place – so we swapped maps with them, giving them a shorter trip and us a longer one. Even so, we made it to the end before them. It was so uneventful it was a bit of a let-down. For a climax to our camping experience, Michael jumped out of our raft to push us across the lake at one point, but otherwise he was much the same as everyone else in the group – competent and a little surprised at how easy it was. This was why we were surprised to get in trouble when we got back to school.

Apparently, we put ourselves and the girls at risk by swapping checkpoints, although I think the real problem was that the teachers following us worked out what we had done a little late, so that there was now a male teacher following the girl's group and a female teacher following us.

Later that year I would also take the road less travelled during the annual 'Lap of the Lake' running event. I hated Lap of the Lake, it was compulsory for all students at the school to take part, and points were awarded to each house based on the order in which you finished, with most points for first, least points for last. For the previous three years I had walked most of it. On this occasion, Michael decided it would be fun to bring his dog Tarzan along, particularly as he might trip a few people up at the start. His plan sort of worked – Tarzan tripped Michael up. This meant that I ran on ahead of him along with hundreds of other runners.

Because we started at the end of Forest Street and ran anticlockwise, we were quickly into the botanic gardens where there are multiple paths. As I was going through one of bushier sections the boarders pulled me aside. In all the confusion Michael and Tarzan ran past. Within the bushy area next to the path were about 20 kids of different ages, mostly boarders. I was told to be quiet and patient as they had a shortcut. Once everyone had gone past, including the supervising teachers, the group used various clumps of trees and shrubs as coverage until we had crossed the road and into one of the suburban streets.

The shortcut turned out to be making away to the street north of the one next to the lake and following it in the opposite direction until we were several blocks on the other side of the finishing line, where the plan was to make our way back to the lake and re-join the race. The difference was we had covered about a sixth of the distance. I was told that this was a secret handed down through the boarding house over many years. The real trick was the timing. Apparently, one year a group had re-joined the race too early and ended up representing the school in the interschool race. Fortunately, someone had set a timer, so we waited for the appropriate amount of time and then re-joined the race in clumps when there was a big enough gap between other runners. We got away with it undetected. Michael was not so fortunate, with no watch on and thinking that I was ahead of him, he had kept running to try and catch me and ended up in the top group of runners, so that he now had to represent the school.

Computing

Year 10 was also when computers arrived at the school. There were two Apple computers, and they had their own room. There was no computer class, and no student below year 10 had access to the computers. Students from year 10 up could book time on the computers, but only after they had done the computer training. In year 10 this was given to all students as part of maths class. The entire training extended across two lessons, so about 90 minutes, and it was focused on how to write computer programs. It instantly made sense to me.

In the same week, I was given lines to write as a punishment by my commerce teacher. He was an elderly teacher that the students referred to as sieve-head because he tended to be forgetful. I have forgotten what the actual words were that I was meant to write. But I do remember writing three lines of code on the computer and watching the printer write my 100 lines and thinking that computers were a good thing. I liked them even more when I handed in the lines and was given a very well done for typing them.

When I told Michael about this, he also became interested in computers, and we would book time in the usually empty computer room to test our skills. I spent time trying to create new things, Michael spent time trying to access things that he was not meant to find. I also had the advantage of having done 'typing' as a subject in year 9, so I could touch type while Michael did the two fingered peck that was common at the time.

Within months of computers arriving at school we had one at home. It was not as good as the ones at school, but it was good enough for Mum's Master's degree. We were not the only ones to have a computer, but all the other kids just used them for computer games. We had no computer games, and so had to create our own.

After writing lines, the next program I recall writing was to calculate how far I had to walk to mow our two acres of lawn. This involved establishing the circumference of the various shapes (including the middle of the circular driveway), and then reducing the circumference by the width of the mower after each lap and adding it all together. Mum still thought I should take less time to do the mowing – this being the point of contention that had me write the program in the first place. But Dad was impressed, and then gave me the dimensions of various paddocks, and the width of the slasher. This gave him the distance the tractor had to travel. Knowing this and the speed of the tractor and rate of fuel consumption per hour, enabled him to calculate the cost of fuel required to mow the paddocks. He then shared this with the agriculture department office in Ballarat, and within a year I was writing computer programs for them as well.

The program that changed the farm was using the formula from the herd performance program created by the University and rewriting it so we could run the program at home. This meant that instead of paying them a fee and waiting several weeks, we could put the numbers in at lunchtime and have the results in the afternoon. This saved the cattle an extra trip through the yards and us a week of cattle yard work – which would have been a lot of money if Dad paid us.

To Dad's credit he was well ahead of his time in adopting herd performance calculations as part of his herd management. Most farmers still relied on a visual assessment of the animals. It was a well-respected skill to be a good judge, and Dad would get us to practice it at home, when we had to try and get the same results as him, as well as at cattle shows, including the Royal Melbourne Show, which we went to every year. At the shows we not only had to try and match his opinion, but we also had to try and match the official judge, and listen to his reasoning afterwards as a form of feedback on how we could get better.

There was also a junior judging competition at the shows, in which young adults had their judging skills tested against one another. Dad was one of the organisers of the cattle competitions at the Ballarat show, and when there were not enough entrants in the junior judging competition, he got Deb to join in. It was a significant decision as it would introduce Deb to her future husband, Steve.

Typical of Deb, she did not hesitate to join in, her attitude even before her operations was to give everything a go. She never worried about success or failure, she just wanted to gain as many experiences as she could. In the 18 months between having her second operation and meeting Steve at the Ballarat show, Deb had already tried three different jobs – the supermarket, the farm and working at the Royal Melbourne Show while staying with Gran Kent.

Her approach to the junior judging competition was simple – she asked the other competitors for help. She came last, which did not phase her, but while talking to Steve she discovered that he had also worked at the Melbourne Show that year and that he lived at Wooloomanata (Mum's parents' old property), where his father was the manager for the new owners. This was enough to get them talking and for Steve to arrange to visit Deb on the next available weekend.

I remember the visit as it was the first time one of us had an official suitor. Barb, Cindy, and I were close enough in age to have our friends date our siblings, but our parents never knew about it. Steve was also an adult and had his own car. He arrived nearly two hours early and parked up the road. We all knew about it because cars were uncommon enough for us to notice them going past, let alone parked in the middle of nowhere for over an hour.

Because they lived two hours apart, the courtship involved them staying with each other's families on alternate weekends. I enjoyed it when Steve came to stay as it was like having a brother. I think Steve enjoyed it for the same reasons as he also had three sisters and no brothers – so we played a lot of sport together, which would have been a relief to my sisters, particularly Barb.

Even though Barb was my younger sister, for the last five years she, like my two older sisters, was physically bigger than me. Even so, she was my best chance of getting someone to play sport with – although she bargained hard. In cricket she would only bat. We had a large lawn, and usually only one fielder, so the rules were that if the ball was hit then you had to run, and when the fielder got to the ball it was the equivalent of hitting the wicket. When Barb refused to bowl or field, we played a set number of deliveries and every time I got her 'out' she lost 10 runs. At the end of any of these games, regardless of the score, I would beg for another game. Barb would head for her bed as though it provided a kind of sanctuary – it didn't.

I would follow her there and wrestle and argue with her trying to convince her to play some more. I rarely succeeded, but it did not stop me trying. But in year 10 the balance of power shifted because during year 10 I grew. In April, at the end of the rowing season, I still weighed 40 kg, but by the start of the next year I was 63 kg and significantly taller. This also meant that my attacks on Barb now had some power behind them. Fortunately, Dad made a timely intervention.

I remember clear as day him stepping into Barb's room while we fought on her bed. He didn't raise his hand nor his voice, he simply said. 'There is always someone bigger, someone smaller, someone smarter, someone dumber – don't get an ego about it'. Then he turned and left the room. His sizeable presence left me in no doubt that he was someone bigger, and his wise words also told me that he was someone smarter. Not long after this, apropos of nothing he said, 'The true test of strength is gentleness'. He then went on to explain how it requires a lot more power and control to raise a heavy weight slowly, or to hold a calve struggling to be free gently.

At some point along the way he also taught me the calf hold, which I have used on toddlers, puppies, and other animals to great effect since. It is quite simple. If they struggle, you hold them a little tighter, if the relax, you give them more space to move. After a few rounds of struggle, they settle down and stop fighting. It also seems to calm them.

Sometimes I would get Cindy to play sport with me, but even when willing she was not a reliable participant. This always confused me. She was skilled on a horse, good at rowing and aerobics, netball, and bike riding, but cricket and tennis were hit and miss. She was also very self-conscious. When serving in tennis she demanded we didn't look – even if we were the person she was serving to. So, we would stand ready to receive the ball with our eyes shut, waiting for the sound of ball hitting racquet before opening our eyes and attempting to return the serve. Often this involved watching the ball fly over our heads and out of the court. At other times she would ace us. Cricket was a bit the same, she would hit sixes or miss the ball completely. She was also prone to losing the balls – which were treasured – particularly the ball we used to play cricket.

It was a tennis ball that we had injected with water to give it more weight. The advantage of this was that it didn't hurt if it hit you, but it also meant you could bowl fast without feeling like you were trying to throw your hand off the end of your arm. The other advantage was that it maintained its momentum on the grassed lawn. Once any of our friends had played with a water filled ball, they wanted to do the same thing at home. That was easy enough for the farm kids, there was generally a syringe and thick needle available on most farms. The city kids would give us tennis balls so that we could inject them and hand them back.

It was during that first summer with Steve and the end of year 10 that he, Barb, and I were having a game of cricket using the pitch in the middle of the lawn. Although pitch is overstating it, it was simply a part of the lawn that I mowed shorter than the rest of it. I only played beach or backyard cricket. In grade six my nose had been broken while fielding in the slips when the batsman threw the bat while attempting to hit the ball. I had tried to avoid playing cricket or hockey since. As much as Dad loved rowing, my key motivation for taking up the sport was avoiding hard balls and bats. Steve on the other hand still played cricket for his local team.

On this occasion Barb did not want to bat, bowl or field, but she was prepared to keep wickets. So, Steve and I took turns at batting. Steve opened the batting for his cricket team and was a competitive person by nature. This combination would prove to be his downfall. As an opening batsman, his instinct was to block the ball, which would have him almost instantly run out. Then during my turn to bat I would swing wildly at the ball, often nicking it through the vacant slips, or skying it to absent fielders. With each shot I would accumulate more runs, while Steve would get more frustrated and try to bowl even faster at me. When I got to 50 runs, I offered to retire, but he was determined to get me out. When I got to 100, I offered to retire again as he was clearly exhausted – but he insisted on playing on. From then I tried to hit catches to him, but I lacked the skill to execute the plan. Then Barb broke the deadlock by saying she wanted to go inside.

Deb rarely played sport with us after her first operation. She was told she should avoid stressful situations, including sport, although Deb rarely got stressed while playing sport, because like the judging competition she didn't really care about the result. After the second operation Deb was more susceptible to what she called 'blanks'. These were described to us as being like an epileptic fit, but Deb's version was different. Deb would lose consciousness but unconsciously continue whatever activity she had been doing when the fit occurred. To understand this, consider walking along while talking to someone or thinking about something else. During these moments you are not conscious of walking. So, if Deb had a fit during one of these moments she would continue walking, but not be conscious of her surroundings.

I remember one occasion when this happened on the farm. We were getting firewood, which happened at least every fortnight during winter. Dad would decide which dead trees we were going to cut down and then one of us would drive the tractor and tip trailer there, while the others went in the Landcruiser with Dad. Once we were all there, Dad would tell us which trees he was going to drop where so we could move ourselves and the vehicles out of the way. He would then start up the larger chainsaw and drop the trees, before we moved the tractor and tip trailer closer and started up the smaller chainsaw and set to work on cutting the fallen trees into firewood and throwing the pieces onto the trailer.

It was during the tree felling that Deb had a blank – unfortunately she was walking at the time. Dad was focused on making sure the tree fell where he intended, and the rest of us were watching from a safe distance when we saw Deb walk into the space where the tree was about to fall. We tried yelling but Dad could not hear us over the chainsaw, and Deb was oblivious to her surroundings. Fortunately, the tree dropped all around Deb without her even getting a scratch – like the famous silent movie scene when the front of a house drops around the actor. After this incident we made sure one of us had contact with Deb when danger was imminent.

Deb moving into adulthood changed the dynamics within the household, particularly as she struggled with full-time work and so needed more rest time. She even sold her milking cows so she could get more sleep. Other chores around the house were also reshuffled. Barb took on more of the kitchen duties, Cindy took care of the animals, and I did the fires and the lawns.

We also moved all the desks into one room, called it a study and the three of us would be sent there every night to do our homework. I think this was done for my benefit as I still had no idea how to study. I treated the time as a kind of detention and found ways to entertain myself with the materials available. One of these was combining a three-sided ruler with a rubber-band to slingshot pencils. I even put a target on the back of the door and would fire pencils from my desk on the other side of the room, with the tip of the pencil conveniently marking where it had hit. Unfortunately,

Barb opened the door to walk back into the room when one of the pencils was in flight and was subsequently hit in the forehead, the tip of the grey pencil breaking off and lodging just under the skin. Cindy was in the room with me at the time and vouched for the accidental nature of the incident. We all agreed not to tell Mum and Dad about it.

The next day the school had other ideas. A teacher noticed the raised welt and grey discoloration and called Mum. The teacher said that Barb would not say how she had got the lump, but in her opinion, it looked like someone had thrown a rock at her. When we got home Mum confronted me and accused me of throwing rocks at Barb. I said that was stupid because even if I had surely Barb would have moved, so Mum decided I must have tied her up. As much as Cindy, Barb and I tried, we could not change her mind. I stopped shooting pencils, and Cindy even took pity on my inability to study and tried to teach me how she did it. But it didn't work – my understanding of the material that was evident in the classroom still did not translate into my test results.

Haddon Fire Brigade

By my year 11, the Haddon Fire Brigade was a competent unit with over 40 members and two fire trucks and a shed under Dad's leadership. It was a significant achievement given where it had started just a few years earlier.

I recall the very start, when the Country Fire Authority agreed to create the brigade based on a petition of the residents and a pledge of people to volunteer. The first step the brigade undertook was to raise money to buy a second-hand truck. Those that donated $1,000 would be granted life membership and never asked to help with fundraising again. The idea was to take the existing firefighting unit, designed to be loaded onto the back of a flat-bed truck when needed, and permanently attach it to the purchased truck. It all made sense, as the existing unit was very rarely used as despite its promise of being ready to go, it would take about an hour to load it onto a truck and secure it.

On closer inspection it also turned out to be faulty. The identified problem was that someone had used it to drain a sheep dip, and so all the pumping equipment was blocked up with wool. We did not have a sheep dip, but some of the other farmers present swapped some accusing looks, before getting on with the task of converting the newly acquired truck and the equipment into a fire truck capable of fighting fires.

For their part the CFA provided a trailer of knapsacks, fire rakes and fire beaters. They also provided a phone number which rang at four houses simultaneously – ours being one of them. Each of the four houses had a list of people to call next, and those people also had lists of people to call. When the CFA installed the Fire Brigade Shed, it also had a siren – which any of the four houses could activate by pushing a button on the phone. This was tested at 10 am every Sunday morning during summer and the first Sunday of the month during the rest of the year.

Like other local farmers, we also had our own firefighting equipment. Ours was a tank the same size as the fire brigade's with similar water pump, hoses, and nozzles. The nozzles were specifically designed for firefighting, able to handle high pressure, but also able to be changed to different settings by twisting them. An important one of these settings being the ability to create a water wall or screen that the operator could use for self-protection, or just as importantly to protect the pump. As we were told very early on, no pump equals no water – so protecting the pump is the highest priority. During summer, this arrangement was mounted on the back of the tip-trailer and connected to the tractor ready to go at a moment's notice. Outside of the fire season the tank was hung from the branch of a large pine tree, while the pump and hoses were stored safely in one of the farm sheds.

Our other key defence against fire was the driveways and lawn. The lack of other vegetation was intentional. The only way a fire could get to our house was by windblown cinders, and for that we had another defence. Research had shown that falling cinders start house fires by falling into the gutters and setting fire to dry leaves, then getting up under the eaves and setting fire to the house from the roof cavity. So, in summer I would clean the gutters every couple of weeks. We also had downpipes that could be blocked so that we could fill the gutters with water. As a result, our house was never in danger.

The opposite was true for many of our newer neighbours. They loved building houses amongst the trees, and even when they built their house on pasture, they almost immediately started planting gum trees and wattle trees around their houses. It was as though they had read the CFA guidelines and decided to do the opposite. They were also prone to panic. When smoke filled the air on one occasion, a newer neighbour was in such a rush to get his horse into the horse float, he drove it too close to the house at high speed, and hit the eve of the house, wrecking the horse float and part of the roof. Fortunately, neither the house nor the horse was in any danger of being burnt by fire.

To help protect the neighbourhood, the fire brigade organised burn offs to create fire breaks. This usually meant burning along the side of key roads, including the main road that ran along the north boundary of the brigade's zone, as well as other roads that dissected it. While none of the roads were more than two lanes wide, and some were gravel, some of the easements were four chains (80 metres) wide. In the early days of the brigade, they had not been burned for decades.

My role in the burn-offs was to drive our firefighting unit (tractor and trailer), usually inside the farmer's paddock, to ensure that the burn-off did not burn their fence or farm. To put this in perspective, burn-offs needed to be done when the grass was dry enough to burn, so usually early or late summer, and on a low wind day. They were planned and the local authorities were informed of the plans. Because they were weather dependent, they were also frequently cancelled. When they did go ahead, it was a very organised event involving at least four firefighting units, including ours.

Two of these would be inside the paddock, two on the road. One of the ones inside the paddock would be wetting down the fence boundary ahead of the fire, the other would be on standby in case the fire spread. On the side of the fence facing the road, there would be two trucks behind the fire mopping up anything that was smouldering as well as helping to put out anything that should not be burning – such as a fence post, roadside post, or the farmer's land. Ahead of these two trucks were two people with firelighters, who would be walking along dragging the firelighters through the long grass, usually with any breeze blowing away from the paddocks and them.

When positioned to mop up fires that had got through the boundary, I got very hot. This was because the tractor offered no protection from the blaze, and the firefighters on the trailer generally fought the flames next to them, not next to me. Given that the roadsides had decades worth of dry undergrowth as well as a few gorse bushes, even the controlled burns could burst into substantial blazes unexpectedly. It was on one of these occasions all the hair on my face and hands burnt. While there were plenty of flames, I don't recall it touching me, just the smell of burnt hair and grit in my eyes – which turned out to be my burnt eyelashes.

I didn't lose the hair on my head because it was covered by a wool beanie. The rest of my body was protected by coveralls, a CFA issue that had extra fire retardants in the fabric. I am still baffled any time I see people at risk of fire wearing almost no clothing. CFA coveralls are ideal, but if you cannot get them then wet wool is best, but it is heavy, so dry wool is the next best thing. After wool is cotton – it burns away from the skin. Worst are nylon and polyester – they melt into the skin. We always had large wool blankets in the cars during summer along with a large water container. The drill, which we never had to use, was to pull the car off the road onto some clear ground. Ideally, face the front of the car at the fire (the engine provides a barrier to the heat of the flames), wet the blanket, and then get under the wet blanket below the height of the windows until the fire passes. The blanket not only protects from the heat, it also acts as an air filter. The other addition to this was to always have matches – so if there was no clear ground, we could set fire to it and then move onto the burnt patch.

A few summers into the brigade's existence we were plagued by a series of deliberately lit fires. As we were always the first to know about the fires, we were also often the first to the fire-sheds. Dad would drop me off and I would get on the back of one of the trucks and get the pump going, meanwhile the first person with a truck licence would be in the driver's seat taking us toward the fire. By the time we could see the flames Dad would have determined how we were going to access them. This often meant he had to cut the wire fence. Sometimes, this also meant that if no one else had shown up, I would be the only one on the back of the truck as we headed into the fire area. Given that we could never see very much, this simply meant putting out the fire nearest me, from the bottom up and from the back to the front. If there were two of us on the truck, we would work as a team, one hitting the hot spots, one sweeping up behind – the key is to make sure it does not restart.

Fairly quickly, there would be other trucks and firefighters helping – working from the back of the fire and down the flanks, always driving on the burnt ground, until those working the flanks converged and the fire was said to be contained. It would not be out until hours, sometimes days later when all the hot spots had been put out. During this summer, the arsonist would often light more than one fire, but always away from houses. The police suspected that it was a member of the fire brigade, and so the captain, Dad, was asked to keep track of any suspicious behaviour.

After some amateur detective work, he reduced it down to a single suspect. There was not enough evidence to charge him, but the police suggested Dad have a chat to him, to let him know that he was now being watched. I don't know how the chat went, but the fires stopped.

I hated fighting fires in the trees, and we did not have any of the big fire ball blazes to deal with. A grass fire is a little claustrophobic because of the lack of visibility, but I found fighting fires in the trees very claustrophobic, not only because the fire has three dimensions, but also because the vehicle is often struggling to find its way. So, there is a constant sense that at any point we could be stuck. The other factor is the noise, an animal like roar combined with the snapping and crashing of timber. I still hate driving through forests in fire season. I much prefer an open expanse, particularly one with views to the north and west (the dangerous summer winds). I also still like a large green lawn, although mowing them is a chore. Mowing the lawn in year 11 was my ticket to the games.

Games and Leadership

The 1982 Commonwealth Games in Brisbane were during my year 11. The school offered us the option of going, but at some cost. My parents agreed that I could go providing I mowed the lawn at least 12 times beforehand. Fortunately, just before this deal was made, Dad had purchased a new mower – the same type that the council works used. It was bigger and self-powered, so while we still had to do the walking, we did not have to do the pushing. This was much better than the little Victa mower designed for a suburban block that could only cope with short grass, and took so long it inspired me to write the computer program to calculate how far we walked. Even then, that calculation did not consider the back and forth required when the going got tough.

I know Mum was keen on the lawn being mowed regularly, and given we never got any pocket money, none of us were keen on mowing it. This meant that it would get long, and once long would be unable to be mowed – at least by the Victa. Dad had some farm solutions for this. One year he put an electric fence around it and put the cattle on it. That did not turn out well. We had hoof prints and cow pats everywhere, and when the lawn had recovered from them, we had weeds from the seeds in the cow dung. Another year Dad enclosed it with temporary fencing and put some sheep on it. The problem this time was that he used the sides of the house as part of the enclosure and the sheep had access to the veranda and the garden beds. Not surprisingly they ate Mum's plants. More surprisingly, one of the rams felt threatened by his own reflection in a full-length window and rammed it, smashing through it and into the house. We were eating breakfast at the time and were a bit startled by our new guest. Fortunately, he was unharmed and was quickly guided back out to the rest of the flock. We then boarded up the window and moved the sheep into a nearby paddock before going to school a few hours late.

The most memorable solution was when Dad decided to let the lawn grow longer and then made hay bales out of it. In the process he clear felled a small garden Mum had made, left numerous tractor marks from the process of mowing, raking, and baling the lawn with heavy machinery – and left the corners uncut. The 80 hay bales were the finest quality rye and clover bails, but the process left the lawn looking like a paddock. It was these heavy tracks and divots that were apparently the reason we did not get a ride on mower. I say apparently because a few years later, after I had left home, they did get a ride on mower – despite the fact that Dad weighed significantly more than me, divots were no longer a concern.

At the start of year 11, with a new mower and a trip to the Commonwealth Games many months away, mowing it 12 times – the equivalent of once a fortnight – seemed a reasonable deal. I would manage it, just, and not without a few shortcuts. Earlier on due to rowing commitments I missed mowing it a couple of times, and so then had some catching up to do. Fortunately, grass does not grow as fast in the winter months, and Mum was never one to wander the lawn. So, when I got down to mowing it once a week, I could do significant shortcuts across the bottom of the lawn unnoticed.

That was typical of my approach to life at the time – an easier way was a better way. At one point the school gave grades with a plus or minus. The grade was for what you had achieved, and the plus or minus was for the effort. I remember having a long argument with Mum about A minus being a better grade than A plus. To my way of thinking if you could get the same result and do less work, then it was a better achievement. Mum was of the view that the plus was more important because it meant you had done your best, and that was all anyone could ask of you. She, like my teachers, found my academic results very frustrating. She thought that I often put more effort into trying to find shortcuts than it would have taken me to do the work.

I found out the hard way that you cannot take shortcuts in rowing. I knew from coxing that I should row as hard and as fast as the rest of the crew. What I found out when rowing was how much it could hurt if you didn't. An oar handle into the stomach when you don't get your blade out of the water in time is soon followed by an oar handle into the back from the person behind you because you are still there. Because of this need for everyone to be in synch, the coach usually puts the fittest most rhythmical rower as stroke (the rower in front of all the other rowers, but furthest from the finish line). I was never that person. Like Deb, I was never a particularly good rower.

That could not be said for Cindy and Barb. In her year 12, Cindy was the stroke for the girls first crew and won the Head of the Lake. A few years later Barb would also win the girls Head of the Lake, and then as a Uni student she would win the National Championship as part of the Melbourne Uni crew. It was a very proud day for Dad, he loved rowing – which I think was the main reason we all did it (apart from me avoiding hard-ball sports).

The Head of the Lake was a big deal. The entire school was required to attend and cheer the teams on against the other Ballarat schools. There were 10 boys races and four girls races at the time, with the earlier races run over a shorter distance with younger crews. In year 11 I rowed in the sevenths, and we came third out of four. Fortunately, this gave us ample time to get the boat back to the sheds and be at the finish line in time for Cindy's race. I remember yelling myself hoarse cheering her on and being so happy for her when she won. I gave her a big hug when she came ashore and cried on my shoulder, as much in relief as joy. The boys crew also won, making the crew I coxed the only one in six years not to have won. But that did not matter, because the other good thing about the Head of the Lake was the ball at school that night. The night started in a much better mood when the crews had won.

The ball was also good in that most of the awkwardness of finding a partner had occurred in the lead-up. This also involved lots of rumours and friends of girls making enquiries as to the chances of a match to try and avoid as much embarrassment as possible. All of these enquiries had been made on my behalf before I asked a girl to my first ball. Even so I was nervous, we were sitting near each other during a whole class assembly, and she had given me a few favourable looks. So as the assembly ended, I went over to ask her to the ball, however the combination of my almost silent enquiry and the loud environment meant that she did not hear me. So, I repeated the question a bit louder, and as luck would have it filled an impromptu quiet moment from the crowd so that everybody heard me this time. Fortunately, she said 'Yes' and gave me a quick kiss on the cheek to ease my obvious embarrassment. Cindy also had a date for the ball, and I recall us being in good spirits before, during and after the event.

Later in the year, on the way to the Commonwealth Games, we were not in such good spirits. Our bus trip was off to a bad start. Less than three hours into the ten-day round trip, we had stopped in Cobram for lunch and were still there four hours later. Our bus had a mechanical problem. We had also had a problem with some of the locals.

We had been playing cricket, using a rubbish bin for a wicket. I was one of the two people batting when four local hoons started heckling us. They had been drinking, and they were taunting the boys and making sleezy remarks at the girls. We just ignored them. This seemed to annoy them and so they came in a bit closer, and some of the kids moved away. Then one of them ran forward and kicked over the bin we were using as a wicket and shaped up to fight me.

I recall thinking that he was an idiot because he could have picked a fight with a dozen other people, and instead he picked on one of two people with a bat. With bat in hand, I waited for him to make the next move, knowing that I had an advantage in range and weapon. I intended to hit a kneecap if he tried anything. Then the school marshal arrived and put his ex-army officer confrontation skills to good use, so that we soon had the park to ourselves. Eventually a replacement bus arrived, and we transferred all our gear into it and continued on our way. The delay meant that our first night of setting up tents in a caravan park had to be done in the dark, and that we missed out on visiting the Sydney Opera House the next day as we sought to make up time.

I don't recall much about the games themselves. In part because we had poor tickets, we were a long way from the action at the athletics and there were only minor heats on when we were at the swimming. But the friendships made on the bus trip by various groups would be long lasting, one romance started on that trip would even result in a marriage many years later. On the first few days the time on the bus seemed very drawn out, but by the end of the trip the hours seemed like no time at all.

None of my closest friends made the trip, but through the recommendation of some of the boarders I had Denby as my tent buddy, and by the end of the trip we would be good friends. I also got to know some of the girls a lot better away from the classroom and without the pressure of dating. The long bus conversations provided some great insights into how they experienced the same classes and people that I experienced in very different ways.

Not long after our return it was time for another Lap of the Lake. Word was out among the boarders that the teachers were onto their shortcut, so the agreed approach was to just do the whole thing slowly. This was a plan I was very comfortable with. So, when a car pulled up and offered us a lift as we were walking about two thirds of the way around, I was quite happy to keep walking. At first, I did not recognise the lads in the car, but Slug and Denby recognised they had been boarders at the school the year before. Slug went over and had a social chat with them. They made the offer several more times before the three of us accepted the lift. From where we got into the car to where we got out probably saved us about a kilometre – we would still be coming in in the bottom third of the competitors, and so really didn't think much about it – just a bit of good luck. But one of the other students we had leap-frogged by taking the lift was put out and would report us to the school.

The next day we were taken to the headmaster and admonished for disrespecting the rules and the school uniform. We were told that our parents would hear about this and that our chances of getting any sort of leadership position at the school were now very slim. Once we were out of the office building and walking back to class, I remember the contrast between Slug and Denby – Slug regarded it as no punishment at all, he had been in trouble numerous times and leadership was not high on his priority list. Denby on the other hand was downcast, I assumed he must have had strict parents, but in retrospect I think it was the leadership he cared more about.

That night my punishment was a topic of conversation around the dinner table. Mum was using it as another example of short-cuts being bad. Dad, who usually enjoyed a good story, was clearly disappointed in me. I thought that everyone was overreacting, then Cindy – who was a house captain – said, 'Don't you realise most people in my year level thought you were going to be school captain next year?'.

A few weeks later Denby and I were given a chance to redeem ourselves. We were both made probationary prefects along with about 20 other students. It was during the year 12 study and exam period, and we were required to take over their prefect duties – which included helping teachers with yard duties at recess and lunchtime and enforcing school uniform standards at the end of the day. I misread the state of play and interpreted the opportunity to prove myself as the school not following through on its punishments. I failed to redeem myself, in fact, even without the prior punishment – I would demonstrate I did not deserve to be a prefect.

At no time in my schooling, other than school assemblies and school photos, did I wear the uniform correctly. I hated wearing the school blazer. Even in winter I would rather put extra clothes under my shirt than wear the blazer for extra warmth. So, while I did wear the blazer when on prefect duty at the end of the day asking others to dress properly, I got a lot of back-chat about the fact that I never did any other time. But what really sealed the case against me being a prefect was a lunchtime yard duty.

On yard duty, prefects patrolled as a boy girl combination, my allocated partner for the year 7 patrol on this hot day was Lisa. Because it was hot, we were not required to wear our blazers, so our prefect badges were not on display. When we arrived at the year 7 courtyard, a water fight was in progress. Two boys had water pistols and were spraying other people, mainly girls, and some of the girls had taken control of the water taps and were spraying them back. They were not keen on listening to us. By the time we got things under control, Lisa and I were both a little wet, and had possession of the water pistols – which turned out to be one water pistol and an oversized syringe (no needle). She kept the water pistol, I kept the syringe. My next class was chemistry, within 30 minutes of the class starting I had the syringe confiscated from me after I had filled it from one of the taps and squirted water on several of my classmates. My teacher was Mr Gray, and when he found out how I had acquired the syringe, he simply shook his head.

When they announced the prefects and school captains a few weeks later I was not one of them. I am pleased to say that Denby was – he had redeemed himself when I had not. I am also pleased that the school did not give me what I did not deserve. I learnt a lot from that.

A few weeks later, the house captains were elected, and I was fortunate to be given the role. More importantly I took the responsibilities of the role seriously, referenced Dad's excellent leadership, and did a job I was proud of. I am not sure I would have done half as well if the school had not been clear that leadership comes at a cost. Denby was also captain of his boarding house – which was a much bigger role and one he would do very well.

Deb's Big Day

In January 1983, a few weeks before I started year 12, Deb got married. It was one of many hot days that summer, with the temperature still being over 40 degrees Celsius well into the evening. The wedding itself was in the school chapel, and I was asked to be an usher. There were more guests for the bride's side, so I was instructed to ask some of them to sit on the other side of the aisle to balance things up.

One of the guests was Deb's brain surgeon Doctor B. I recall talking to him at the reception, he had a good sense of humour and seemed to have a genuine care and affection for Deb. I remember asking him if he went to many patients' weddings, the pause before the response was full of sorrow, then he said, 'Unfortunately not'. At the time I thought it was disappointment at the lack of invites but given that the survival rate from brain cancer at the time was only one in five, and most of the survivors often had to live with serious health issues, I think he was reflecting on how few of his patients had the opportunity to marry. Deb would have an annual check-up with him until he retired, along with another round of surgery in her early thirties. They still write letters to each other.

The other thing I remember was talking to Steve's best man. He was pretty laid back in a country kind of way. I recall him saying he was surprised that Steve had asked him to be his best man, because he didn't really know Steve that well. Then he went on to explain that they had been at school together with a shared group of mates, but the four guys closest to Steve had all died in three separate car accidents. Steve had never mentioned it.

I have no idea where they went on their honeymoon, but when they returned they moved into a worker's cottage on a property near Greendale, about halfway from Ballarat to Melbourne. The good thing about that was that any time we were going to Melbourne we could drop in and see them.

The main reason we went to Melbourne was to watch Hawthorn play. The earliest game I remember going to was the 1975 Grand Final which Hawthorn lost. That day it was just Dad and I because at the time, Cindy and Deb barracked for Collingwood and Richmond respectively and Barb didn't really barrack for anyone. For the 1976 Grand Final, Dad had three tickets, he told Deb she could only come if she barracked for Hawthorn. She did, not just that day, but every day since.

The frequency of trips increased in 1978, the year after Deb's first operation. I think there were several reasons for this, one being that it was something Deb really enjoyed, another was that Mum wanted the house to herself. In typical Dad style the football trips were not just the four kids, we all got to invite a friend. So, it was Dad and eight kids into a station wagon, with two of us in the boot. In the morning we would make up rolls and pack snacks and a thermos. If we were going to a suburban ground, we would also pack seating – which was some flat-top fold-out champ chairs and a plank of wood, (the plank of wood would be put across the chairs to create a bench seat). When the game was on, we would stand on the plank of wood so that we could see.

We left home mid-morning, collected the various friends along the way and generally got to the game at least 90 minutes before it started. This meant we got a decent choice of seating – Dad always liked to be on the forward flank. We would then sit down and watch the reserves game while we ate the food we had prepared. We usually only went to the games between Hawthorn and other top teams, along with Collingwood (for Cindy) and Essendon (for Tony) regardless of where they were on the ladder. Once Deb got married, she would bring tins of cookies and 'hedgehog' slice that she had prepared – we loved them.

The group of kids that went to the football was often the same as those that stayed on the farm during the holidays, so we all knew each other well and enjoyed each other's company. While I have always watched team sport with the eye of a coach, not everyone else did. Dad watched the players and would often ask me what the bigger patterns were. Barb hardly watched at all, often bringing a book. After the game we would get fish and chips in Bacchus Marsh and eat it in the car in the dark on the way home.

If it was finals, we would also go to the Melbourne Show on the way home – Dad had a member's pass which let kids in for free, and we would time it to see the fireworks display and the Holden stunt cars. Sometimes we would get showbags, but we rarely went on rides. Dad would give us a little bit of money and we would agree to meet back at the same spot in a certain amount of time, then we would head off in pairs to explore the showgrounds – which always seemed more interesting in the dark. Win, lose or draw it was always a good day out. In 1983 Hawthorn would win the Grand Final over Essendon, with the regular crew watching on, and everyone – except for Tony – was very happy about the result.

But the year did not start out so happy. It was a hot dry summer – fires were a constant threat and there was barely enough grass for haymaking. Fortunately, we had the irrigation paddock. But a sign of how dry things were, we needed to use the irrigation before Christmas when that paddock was usually lush with grass ready to be cut for haymaking. The waterhole that had a spring in the bottom would be drained three times that summer.

Instead of driving tractors to cut grass for hay, I would be seed drilling millet into the irrigation paddock. This seed drill was attached to the back of the tractor by the hydraulic arms. When seeding it was pushed into the ground so that the curved tines would ripe a channel in the soil, the seed would be dropped into the channel and then a roller at the back would close it over. Because of the drag of the device, steering was done using the split brakes. Like the brakes on most tractors, there were two brake pedals, a left and a right that for most of the time were joined together by a simple latch, so that they worked as one. To activate the separate use was a simple matter of undoing the latch. Because the device could be raised off the ground and driven, the tractor went home at the end of each session.

Unfortunately, at the end of one of these sessions I forgot to re-join the brakes. Fortunately, I was still in the paddock when I applied the right brake while traveling at speed. The damp drilled ground allowed the tractor to slide as it spun. That, combined with the weight of the device on the back, was enough to counter-balance the engine and some quick reflexes prevented the tractor from flipping. Rolled tractors were a major cause of death on farms.

The irrigation paddock and our lawn were the only patches of green on the farm, with every gust of wind being thick with dust. In early February, on Barb's birthday, a dust storm would roll across the state and cover Melbourne in dust. A week later many parts of the state would be on fire on Ash Wednesday.

Luck was on the side of the Haddon Fire Brigade that summer, and we had a relatively incident free fire season, although the brigade was called to help other brigades all too often. This was true particularly during the Ash Wednesday fires, and while we were not directly affected, the sky was full of smoke and the sunset had a strange glow. Like most brigades, one of our trucks had been sent with two crews to help fight fires elsewhere, while we fielded multiple false alarms of fires on the horizon. It was a tough few days for many of the boarders at school as they waited to hear how their homes, farms and neighbours had fared during the fires. Joe's farm was one of the ones burnt along with the neighbouring town. Fortunately, his home and his grandparents' home nearby had both been saved.

Tragedy would strike Joe later in the year when his father was killed in a car accident. He was driving between different parts of their farm when struck by a large truck travelling at speed. Joe would end up putting his plans of going to university to become a vet on hold to go home and help run the farm for a year.

Due to the ever-shrinking lake, the Head of the Lake was brought forward by a month, and the finish line moved out, so that the spectators only saw the boats after the finish line. I was in the thirds that year, and our stroke was a long-distance runner. Because of him we won by over a length in a record time for a third crew. The only reason I was still rowing over the last 200 metres was because I knew that stopping would hurt even more. For the first time in my life, I was completely and utterly spent. I had found a new benchmark in what I was capable of. The other thing I remember was that within half an hour I was fine.

Things were not so fine for Cindy. She had been admitted into architecture at RMIT and moved into Trinity College at Melbourne University. Then on the first day of her course, she was told that there had been a glitch in the enrolment system and that the class was over-enrolled, and that half would need to either defer, or relocate to another university for the year. She was one of the 50% that had to find an alternative. Her alternative was to relocate to Launceston in Tasmania, away from family and friends.

Cindy has always worn her heart on her sleeve, and this was a huge deal for her. She was extremely homesick and would call home often just to hear our voices. Because our school year was three terms long, and she was studying in semesters, it was arranged that I would visit her during the September holidays. It was my first time on a commercial plane. I had previously been up in a small plane and flown over the farm, but this was quite a bit different.

Having flown many times since, there are several things about flying at that time that are worth pointing out. Firstly, there were no security checks. Catching a plane had as much security as catching a bus or a train. Secondly, there was no entertainment or handheld devices, so people talked to each other. Finally, there was a genuine respect and good will between the cabin crew and the passengers.

My stay with Cindy was also memorable. She stayed in dorms that were also used by the nurses at the hospital, and her boyfriend (and future husband), Andrew also stayed there. By the time of my visit, Cindy was a lot less homesick, mostly because of Andrew. I would stay about a week and spend time with Cindy and her friends, and even her classmates. Cindy managed to talk one of her lecturers into letting me accompany them on a field trip to a country school for which the class was going to have an assignment of designing a new playground.

The class fitted into a small bus which was driven by the lecturer. He had a European accent and seemed to enjoy driving fast along the winding wet roads. At one point we approached a hitchhiker and the bus debated whether to give him a lift. The lecturer gave a sharp "No" in a thick accent then took delight in driving through a puddle so that he covered the hitchhiker with water.

I also went to a 21st birthday party on the north-west coast. There were eight of us in a Kombi van – the couple who owned it were in the front, the rest of us sprawled out on the bedding in the back. We had set out early and did a pub-crawl along the way as well as stopping at what the couple regarded as memorable places. We thought they might be scenic, but quite a few of them were just places they had parked the van and made happy memories.

The final adventure was going skiing. While snow had come to Ballarat numerous times in my life, it rarely lasted to the end of the day. This was my first time going to the snow. Cindy and Andrew were better skiers that me, and we were soon parted. At some point during the day, I found a much smaller skier who was about my standard, and although we never spoke, we took turns following each other down the runs. We would even stop and wait for the other person if they fell over – it was a really enjoyable few hours. We parted when I caught up with Cindy and Andrew over food. After the break I was following some other skiers down a run when one of them dropped their stock. It landed handle first in the snow with the sharper end pointing at me. It ended up embedded in my thigh – I still have the scar.

That it was such an action-packed visit was typical of Cindy. She always tried to fit more into a given day than anyone else thought was possible, and she would do it day after day, constantly reorganising the day to squeeze more into it, or to adjust for the extra time taken talking to someone that had not been on the schedule.

Back at home we had another visitor helping to fill the void left by Cindy and Deb departing. Our cousin Sarah was staying with us while studying nursing at the local university. Sarah was a long-time favourite cousin of mine. I had even named several of my pet dogs after her. Sarah had Dad's temperament – a no-fuss approach to life and a rich sense of humour.

Like Dad, she was also happy to give things a go. On a previous stay this had included playing football in the hall with Tony and Cindy. I don't recall who was on which team, but I do remember Sarah kicking the ball (one of my soft toys, a hippopotamus) and getting Tony's finger instead, breaking it. Sarah and Dad also got along well.

Because of the dry year and lack of grass, even when the rains came, we had to feed out more hay than usual. For this task Dad got Sarah and I to help. Because we had to fit this in around a school day, or uni day for Sarah, we would load the trailer the night before and feed it out in the morning, before getting ready for school. After one of these evening loading sessions, we were late for dinner, so there were only the three of us at the table. Having finished the meal, Dad asked Sarah and I if we would like some ice cream as he took our plates to the kitchen. We said yes, then he put his head back in around the door and asked if we would like topping and nuts as well. We both said yes to that and went back to chatting. Then we heard some hammering in the kitchen and wondered what was going on. Then Dad appeared with our ice cream, decorated with flavoured topping and some pulverised salted mixed nuts. We exchanged smiles as we ate a memorable dessert.

Year 12

The final year of school is always going to be a big deal, even before all the teachers tell you that your results will determine the rest of your life. 1983 was also the year AIDS started to get some media attention. In our year level, sexual promiscuity had already taken a hit from a graphic arts class a few years earlier.

The class was provided with lots of second-hand magazines so that we could cut them up and make collages on various themes. That exercise was not the issue, it was that some of the magazines were *Cleo*, a women's magazine that was attempting to strike back against sexism by introducing a naked male centrefold and a sealed section. In the class the centrefold was no big deal, but one of the sealed sections was on sexually transmitted diseases – with detailed photos in full colour. As with anything shocking and uncomfortable at school at the time – it was immediately shown to as many people as possible. Subsequently, we all took a much more conservative approach to sex than was generally expected from kids growing up in the 'free love' era.

People's sexuality or sexual preference were not discussed, perhaps it was a country thing, but it was all quite simple. Sexual preference was similar to colour preference or choice of football team to follow – it was known to exist and not expected to be swayed by argument. The rules of engagement were also simple – if you were keen on someone you could ask them if it was reciprocal – and if not, you had to respect that.

Some people, boys usually, had trouble with that last bit. They say that love is blind, but someone with hurt feelings can be dumb as well. A common comeback from a boy rejected by a girl was to call her a 'slut'. Which is mindbogglingly stupid – a slut was a girl that lacked discernment in her choice of partners and subsequently had many of them – so for a boy to conclude on the evidence that a girl didn't want to go out with him that she was the sort of girl to go out with everyone else defies reason. But logic was not really the point – being labelled a slut was bad news for a girl – so the sole intent was to cause harm. No doubt this caused genuine pain, but also reinforced the girls resolve that she had made the right decision. What some guys didn't realise is that girls tell each other much more about their encounters with boys than boys say about girls – so treating one girl badly has a serious knock-on effect. In year 12 I regarded lots of girls as my friends but did not have a girlfriend – which is not to say I was not tempted or courted.

There were two things that put me off the idea. One was that I was afraid of rejection – but that could not have been all of it, because I even baulked on certainty. The bigger reason was Mum's attitude to teen romance. A few years earlier I had stayed back after school to be with a girlfriend while Cindy was playing sport. When Mum arrived to pick us up, I was nowhere to be found. I had lost track of time, so by the time I got in the car Mum was in a mood and on a rant. She left me in no doubt that she felt that I had not only been wasting my time, but now hers for some pointless puppy love that would pass faster than it began. I also knew how she felt about us spending time on the phone. Lisa had called me up one time for a friendly chat – which was the thing to do before the internet and social media – Mum had interrupted every couple of minutes to tell us to get off the phone. In these circumstances I could not see how I could have the sort of relationship and commitment that I witnessed some of my friends have with their partners.

Year 12 also saw Michael and I reunited in English – we had both dropped down to the C class, David remained in B and by now the hard-working Lisa was up in A. When we found out we were in C we were initially saddened, not by the change in status, but because we had Mrs R. She had a reputation for being tough and uncompromising and we were expecting to be in for a long year. Our initial experience in her class was consistent with her reputation – then Michael made a breakthrough.

We had been set a homework task with the warning that she would know by the look on our faces at the start of the next class who had not done it. Michael had not done the homework, but he had grabbed a cardboard box from somewhere and put it over his head while waiting for Mrs R to enter the room. We all saw her smile, before telling Michael to take the box off his head. Knowing she had a sense of humour changed the mood of the class. We also began to realise that she was making us better at English. She also gave me something I had lost a few years before, the confidence to express myself in writing.

She acknowledged that my handwriting and spelling were awful, that was a simple statement of fact. But she had taken the trouble to look through the almost opaque screen that they created and liked what she found. With a word processor on the computer at home, I was able to share my writing unhindered, and she provided me with feedback and encouragement. Unfortunately, the end of year exam was handwritten, and my handwriting and poor spelling combined to hide whatever talent may have been present in full camouflage. When I got my results, I was disappointed for me, but devastated for Mrs R. All her efforts deserved better. Within 10 years of finishing school, I had written over 100 articles published in business and computer magazines. Mrs R was still teaching at the school, so I wrote to her to thank her. More than anything I wanted her to know that her efforts were not wasted.

Mrs R was not the only teacher who left a legacy. Mr V taught year 12 economics, which coincided with my study periods. Still clueless on how to study, I would either distract other students from their studies or join his class. I found economics fascinating, but it involved too much writing for me to consider doing it as a subject. But Mr V encouraged me to join the class, particularly for the discussion sessions. Many years later I would write an economics website www.honesteconomics.com to help explain economics to those who have not been trained in it.

Mr Gray was my chemistry teacher in year 12, he was also one of the rowing coaches, and more importantly a mentor. The first crew that year were big and loud, with Moose at the centre of their antics. On the rowing trips I would prefer to travel in the school Landcruiser that towed the boats driven by Mr Gray. We had some great conversations, and he helped me to explore what career I might want to have after school finished.

The other teacher that would leave a lasting imprint on me was my football coach, he had been my metalworks teacher a few years earlier and had a well-earned reputation for being laid back. With his support I learnt to coach, something I have enjoyed doing for most of my adult life.

Even though I understood Australian Rules Football very well, up until year 12 I had not been particularly good at it. Until year 10 I was too small, and in years 10 and 11 I was growing so fast I had the coordination of a puppy. In year 12 I was a decent size, fit and trusted my subconscious to do the calculations for me. This last bit might sound a bit strange, but I was also doing physics, so I knew all the maths that needed to go into calculating how hard to kick a ball to a moving target while running and with the wind blowing. On the field I simply did not think about it, and I was an unerringly good left foot kick, (I did not kick with my right foot at all). In a similar vein I could read where the ball was going as it was kicked by others. What I lacked at the start of the season was confidence.

Two things turned that around. One was that as vice-captain I helped to select the team. The more the season went on the more the coach listened to me, and the more often we won. The second thing that occurred was that I flew for a mark, missed it, gave away a free-kick and the coach did not tell me off. I could now play without fear of mistakes. Until that point, I had not realised how inhibiting that had been. Before that match was over, I had taken several intercept marks and kicked a late goal to bring us within two points of winning the game. The following week I was the stand-in captain and played a blinder, taking multiple intercept marks and being easily the best on ground. At the end of the season, I would win the best and fairest. None of it would have happened without the coach giving me permission to try and fail.

So many coaches at the time would drag a player from the field if they did something wrong, which only encouraged them to do nothing at all. To make the coach's life easier, they would also put the marginal players in positions nearest them, often the flanks, so that they could get them off the ground more readily. What was ingrained in the team that year was the idea that effort would be acknowledged, skill errors accommodated, and team play valued over individual flair. Even those outside the team recognised that we had a good thing going and wanted to join in. We had a great year, and I had a blueprint for coaching, which works just as well on soccer and netball.

The last part of year 12 was less fun. Teachers were ramping up the importance of exams and results, classmates were feeling the pressure, and underneath it all was a growing realisation that it all was about to come to an end. All too soon the great friendships and fun times would just be memories. Then there are the big assessments and assignments, which seem to get more numerous and more important.

In chemistry, most of the assessment and assignments were in class labs, and I was blessed with my allocated lab partner. Susan was in the top three students in the school, I think she was meant to be a good influence on me. As for my contribution to her work, all I can say is that I kept her entertained. One incident was indicative of our lab work. It was a dangerous experiment in which protective clothing and the fume cabinet was required. We agreed that I would wear the protective clothing and she would tell me what to do from a distance. This started out okay, although the protective clothing was one size fits all, which meant that it did not fit anyone. So, there was a constant battle to do the fine motor skills required as part of the experiment while wearing ill-fitting gloves, mask and so forth. Occasionally Susan would break protocol and step in to help things along. The further we got into the experiment the more this happened until I was standing behind her in the full hazard gear while she completed the experiment without any protective equipment at all.

In geography there was one major assessment, which was a research assignment. My topic was the impact of gold mining on farming, using our farm as the case study. Fortunately, Cindy was home the week it was due, and she worked on it with me well into the early hours of Friday morning (the day it was due). At this point she managed to convince me that staying up all night was easier than getting a small amount of sleep – I believed her. So, we stayed up talking, before I got ready for the school day – which happened to be the house sports carnival.

As house captain I was obliged to find contestants for all the events. In my age group that often meant me. So, on no sleep I would run the 1,500 metres, the 400 metres, do the triple jump, long jump and 100 metre relay. I can't recall the results, but I was exhausted. Dad picked us up and when he stopped outside the supermarket on the way home, I went to sleep. He could not wake me when we got home, so he carried me to bed. I would eventually wake up 16 hours after going to sleep. My recommendation to anyone is get sleep whenever you can.

My final exam was physics on November 23rd – the day before Deb gave birth to baby Laura in a hospital in Ballarat. So, with all the insensitivity and lack of understanding of a teenage boy, I took a bunch of my classmates to visit them on our way to the pub. We all quickly realised that a bunch of schoolboys are not welcome visitors in a maternity ward, so our stay was short.

That I was still at least nine months from my 18th birthday and going to the pub did not seem to be an issue for anyone. Providing someone was old enough to buy the alcohol it became their responsibility who they gave it to. The next day a group of us, mostly boarders, went to Anglesea for the week in what would now be called 'schoolies' – it was just a holiday with mates at the time. Two of my friends were 18 and had driver's licences and cars. We spent the week drinking too much, eating badly, swimming and getting sunburnt on the surf beach – we loved it.

We would return to school for Speech Night, when we would say our goodbyes to lots of friends thinking that we would see them again, only much later realising that we never did. I am sure this happens at most schools, but at a boarding school that has a catchment area bigger than most European countries, it was particularly true. There were no mobile phones or social media and for lots of the boarders we had no idea what their home address or phone number was. It was also a night to say goodbye to the teachers.

A few weeks later we would get our results. Mine were not great, not that I was expecting them to be, but certainty quashes hope very quickly. For most of my friends there were no real surprises. Slug never expected to do well and was already settled into life on the farm. Joe got into vet science and deferred for the year, and just about everyone else got into the course they wanted, mostly in Melbourne. Michael got into commerce in Ballarat and would have a career in accounting – no joke.

Summer Fun and the Long Goodbye

Before making any career decisions I had a job to do. After haymaking had finished, another friend of mine Campbell and I had been hired by Dad to complete the subdivision fencing. The fact we were fencing more subdivision was a sign of another bad year on the farm. It was now almost half the maximum size it had once been. Campbell was starting his career as a wool classer in a few months and was a well-grounded country kid. Most of the fence posts had been pole driven into position by a contractor. Our job was to put in the strainers, drill the posts, run the wires, and pull them tight. We were being paid for the completed job and splitting it half each – so efficiency was to be prized.

The first strainer-end took us two hours, and we had twenty of them to do. To give some idea of the task, a strainer-end has four key components. The strainer post, which is the larger post that the gate swings from, and anchors one end of a taut wire fence. They are four times bigger and heaver that the other fence posts. Then there is also a normal fence post that is positioned along the fence line exactly the length of the strainer pole away from the strainer post. The other key component is the cross bracing which is two laps of fencing wire on a 45 degree angle that pulls the two posts and the pole tightly together. We had a post-hole digger on the back of the tractor, but it was summer, the ground was hard, and the hole it created was narrower than the width of the strainer. The rest of the hole needed to be dug with crowbar and shovel. At the end of those two hours, we thought we were going to be working very hard for our money. Fortunately, we got better and faster, before the week was out, we had it down to 30 minutes, and the last ones we did would have taken us around 20 minutes. In the process I uncovered that I was not inherently lazy, I was just a little obsessive about efficiency.

What made the few weeks more fun was that Campbell had brought his motor-cross bike with him. The only motorbike I had ever ridden was a mini-bike in Michael's suburban driveway. The first time I did was nearly the last. I got on the bike at the rear of his driveway and drove toward the street, which was a main road with lots of traffic. As I reached for the handbrake, I accidently accelerated. With the end of the driveway rapidly approaching, I turned sharply to the right and put my right foot on the ground. This took some weight off the rear wheel and so it spun sharply so that I completed a 180 degree turn with the throttle down and was rocketing back toward Michael. He said that he thought I was showing off until he saw the look on my face.

Campbell's bike was bigger, and so was the space we had to ride it in. On the way to and from the fencing job, we would take turns at driving the tractor or riding the bike. With the person on the bike taking detours and having fun, while the tractor went slowly and steadily towards its destination pulling a trailer weighed down with fencing equipment. After one of his detours Campbell described how he had found a rise over which he could get the bike airborne. He described roughly where it was and how to stand on the bike while airborne and landing. He also emphasised the need for speed.

The next few times we swapped turns on the bike, we discussed how to get airborne. I had explained how my first attempt had been too slow and how I had stuck to the ground, but now I was going full throttle and jumping about 10 metres. Campbell said that it would just feel like that far, although I could be going further than him because I was lighter. So, the next time he came to watch. Apparently, I was wrong, not just about the distance, but my choice of rise. By this time, I had jumped it more than a handful of times and was quite comfortable about it – until Campbell said that I was crazy as I was launching myself off a ski jump-like slope and going at least 20 metres in the air before landing. It was the last time I did it – I did not want my accidental achievement to become an accident.

That summer Dad and I also had an unspoken misunderstanding which I have long regretted. Not about a specific incident, but on what the objective was for the work we were doing together. My understanding of the objective was to get stuff done, and for me that meant as efficiently as possible. Dad's understanding of the objective was to do stuff while we spent time together – but he never said that. So, I would look at the task list for the day and reorganise it to be more efficient and get a sad puppy look from Dad – particularly if it meant doing stuff apart.

Part of the reason I was trying to be more efficient was to get stuff done so I could spend time away from the farm. Dad kept calling me home to help with work, and I kept wondering why he needed me. I did manage to visit my cousins in Adelaide, Kate and Robin. I really liked both of them, but at the time they did not like each other much. They were two sisters trying to hammer out a new relationship as they transitioned into adulthood. Kate was older but smaller, I was in between them in age, but at family functions had always spent more time with Robin. She had a great sense of humour, while Kate had a tremendous inner drive. At the time of my visit Kate was training for an international sailing competition for a two-person catamaran called a 'Tornado'. She was super fit, and although petite, was super strong. I recall walking past her doing weights with barbells one morning on my way to breakfast. On my way back she was gone so I thought I would have a go – I could hardly lift what she had just been doing casual repetitions with. I also got to go sailing with her. I simply followed instructions, rushing from one side of the boat to the other and flinging myself out on the trapeze as a counterweight. It was great fun.

Back on the farm Cindy was home for the summer, and one of her friends Corina had a car and loved going to the one-day cricket to watch Australia and the West Indies. It was when Viv Richards was in his prime, and the games were very entertaining. It was also about this time that she got sad because Dad started calling her Corina. Dad was bad with names, and when Corina first came to stay, he called her multiple names until somehow landing on Elsbeth, so for six years he had called her Elsbeth. Now, Corina was sad to be losing her pet-name.

Not everyone took being called the wrong name well. As previously mentioned, Dad was often put in charge of things – this included being president of the Haddon tennis club. At one of the meetings, he forgot the female treasurer's name and referred to her as 'darling'. She took offence to this and told him that she was definitely not his darling and demanded an official apology be recorded in the minutes. In a small community this sort of news gets around and so for years afterwards numerous local women would refer to Dad as 'darling' and give him a smile and a wink. I am not sure what this did to Dad's reputation with people who were new to the neighbourhood.

Meanwhile on the farm our misunderstanding continued, and tension built around what university course I was going to do. I had originally wanted to be a physical education teacher, but my grandmother was trying to talk me out of it. She told me not to make a hobby into work, that a good friend of hers had loved music until she became a music teacher. My other option was computer science, although I was not sure I was ready for an indoor job. In the end it came down to location. If I did phys ed then I would be living at home, while computer science would be in Melbourne. I compared Sarah's time with us to my time spent with Cindy in Tasmania and picked the one that was away from home.

With this decision made I needed to enrol and to find a place to stay. Fortunately for me, Tony had not liked his original choice of university course and was now enrolling at the same place I was – Rusden Campus of Victoria College, which was next door to Monash

University. He also suggested that Mannix College – one of the Monash University student residences, would be a good place to stay. I remember enrolling at the same time as Tony, and then making a second trip for my interview with the Mannix principal. The main reason I remember the interview is that I had been stung between my toes by a bee when running across the lawn the day before. I had an allergic reaction and now my foot up to the ankle was about three times its normal size. The doctor had told me that I had to keep it elevated as much as possible. So, I rested it on the dashboard on the drive down, and when the condition was explained to the principal, he told me to put my foot up on his desk. As a result, I had my first official interview of any kind with my bare foot on the interviewer's desk.

A few weeks after the interview, I was back at Mannix ready to move in. The room was like every other room in the college. It had its own sink on the open side of the door, a walk-in robe behind the door, and an open space with a hydronic heater under an aluminium sash window. It also had a desk and a single bed, and a bookshelf installed on one wall. Mannix would be my home away from home for the next two years, and in that time, I saw at least a dozen different arrangements of the room, with additions of plants and fridges and other odds and ends.

On this day I simply had lots of clothes and books. I was greeted by some of the other students, including several of Cindy's friends from Grammar and I was invited to join them and some other students for drinks in one of the rooms whenever I was ready. Dad suggested we get some toiletries and cleaning equipment for the sink first and so I let them know I would see them soon. Dad and I then went to 7-Eleven and got the various things he thought I would find useful including some food items. We took them up to my room, and then I walked him down to the car thinking more about what was ahead of me than what I was leaving behind.

Dad was in no hurry to say goodbye, he triple-checked that I had everything I needed. He hugged me extra hard and had a tear in his eye as he got into the car. I walked back into the building and up the stairs to join the other students. With the ignorance of youth, I had no idea that I was leaving behind an awesome childhood made extra special by the man who was driving away.

Author's Notes

As I mentioned at the start, this recollection is as accurate as my memory allows. It does not include everything I remember as I tried not to tell other people's stories. That there is less on Mum and Barb than the others is more a reflection of their preference for privacy than any lack of involvement or influence in my life. Indeed as an adult I have often reflected that my adult self would more often agree with Mum that with the younger me on several of the issues we argued about.

I have tried to use nicknames or initials to protect the adults that the children in this story have become, but the people and events are as I recall them. If you know some of the people in this story and they have a different recollection, treat them as equally valid. What I have shared of my own thoughts and character I hope helped you absorb the experience and to understand that it was the childhood, not the child that was special.

Notes on Location

If you look up Haddon on Google maps you will find several roads and courts named after my family members. The blocks to the south of Kent Road are the ones that Campbell and I fenced. Kathleen, Deborah, Cynthia and Barbara Courts are named after my mum and sisters and are spread across the paddocks we called Cattle Yard 1, 2 and 3 as well as Log Cabin 1, 2 and 3. These were west of the Cattle Yard paddock, which had the yards in it, and Log Cabin paddock, which had the log cabin in it. South of those are three steeper paddocks that were also part of the farm, and west of that was the bush block, through which Andrew Drive runs. That was not named after me, but Murray's son by the same name.

Many of the other road names also made more sense at the time. Haddon School Road was the road the school was on, as well as the driveway to our house. The Taylors lived on Taylors Road, the Wilsons on Wilsons Road, the Kopkes on Kopke Road. Ross Creek–Haddon Road went between Ross Creek and Haddon. Some of this is because before more people moved into the neighbourhood most of the roads were not sealed or named and so were referred to by locals by function or association. Others like Blackberry Lane was a lane in name only, with a winding sequence of wheel ruts threading its way through trees and scrub the only track along what was our back fence.

www.ingramcontent.com/pod-product-compliance
Lightning Source LLC
Chambersburg PA
CBHW052355030726
47599CB00014B/1073